MYSTIC CLOUD WALKER

earth walk

MYSTIC CLOUD WALKER

earth walk

BY PATRICIA PEPER TRUMAN

Park Point
PRESS

Park Point Press is an imprint of Centers for Spiritual Living
573 Park Point Drive | Golden CO 80401

Mystic Cloud Walker earth walk
Copyright © 2021, Patricia P. Truman

Park Point Press
573 Park Point Drive
Golden, CO 80401-7402
720-496-1370
www.csl.org/publications/books
www.scienceofmind.com/publish-your-book

Printed in the United States of America
Published October 2021

Editor: Gail Riena Michael

ISBN ebook: 978-1-956198-08-9
ISBN paperback: 978-1-956198-10-2

IN PRAISE OF
MYSTIC CLOUD WALKER:
earth walk

The Reverend Patty Truman is a walker in the heights and the depths of the human experience. In her work and travels, we enter realms of mind and soul that show us that, indeed, the human heart can go to the lengths of God.

— **Jean Houston, Ph.D.**
scholar, philosopher, teacher of wisdom, researcher in human capacities, advisor to UNICEF and author of twenty-six books, including *Jump Time, A Passion for Possibilities,* and *Search for the Beloved.* www.jeanhouston.com

Reverend Patricia and I have traveled on our spiritual and physical journey together for the past twenty-five-plus years. Together we have visited many sacred and beautiful places—India, Thailand, Russia, New Zealand, Australia, Canada, and many more. Patty always has her eyes, mind, and heart open to the beauty and the wisdom gleaned from each destination, and that is reflected in her sacred and deep-feeling poetry. She writes straight from a well of love, compassion, and respect for our precious planet and all creatures who dwell upon it, be it human or animal. Her poetry is a thing of beauty and is in rhythm with the entire Universe.

— **Reverend Judee A. Chapman**
Center for Spiritual Living Capistrano Valley and CFO, Mark Optics Inc.

Patricia Truman doesn't just write from her heart but from her very soul. In a world fraught with busyness, her words remind us of what is truly essential.

— **Jean Hastings Ardell**
author of *Breaking into Baseball: Women and the National Pastime* and coauthor with Ila Jane Borders of *Making My Pitch: A Woman's Baseball Odyssey.* www.JeanArdell.com

I often read and ponder your wonderful works. It struck me that everyone from all walks of life can connect and be touched by your experiences and the powerful emotions written in each poem. This poetry radiates with great thought of the present, past, and future. Sharing with your readers your personal life experiences allows each person to think and connect to your most powerful universal words. A genius work of art!

— **Lord Ricki Landers Friedlander**
music and film producer and a lifelong member of both the Lord Byron Poet Society and the Oscar Wilde Literary Foundation. He is a collector of first-edition poetry books written in the 18th and 19th centuries.

Patricia Truman's sustained spiritual practice manifested this profound volume of poetry, Mystic Cloud Walker. *A Science of Mind practitioner and ordained minister, Rev. Truman allows the One Mind to flow through her into the passages on the page. You will indeed find Divine inspiration here, for it channels through her. You will also discover that the One Mind has a social consciousness and physical tenderness and yearning. Her poetry is an invitation not to just walk one mile in her moccasins, but to travel the world with her to visit sacred sites in walking shoes, to don sturdy hiking boots to tackle challenging terrain, to strap on sandals to traverse the warm sand, to dip bare toes in the ocean, to cultivate the garden in sneakers, and to sizzle on stage in stilettos. This may prove to be a rediscovery of the natural and the familiar, of beauty surrounding you that you have ceased to see, of an inner urging to transcend and commune with the Infinite. Please accept this invitation to join this journey of a lifetime with this amazing poet.*

— **Adrian S. Windsor, Ph.D.**
professor of English and Humanities, ordained minister of Religious Science, author of four books, president of McGregor Wood LLC, and devoted friend of Rev. Patricia Truman

In a free-form writing style that uniquely creates its own journey, Patty Truman unveils a peripatetic soul, both consciously and subliminally, that connects the steps of her feet to the beats of her heart to the personal yet universal thoughts of her mind. With every step, she creates a lyrical rhythm of compassionate wisdom and insight, reminding us to take pause, take note, and appreciate the connection of the natural world to the human spirit and the divinity that drives us onward.

— **Tammy Lechner**
photojournalist for the Los Angeles Times, adjunct professor of English, Chapman University, and affiliate professor of writing pedagogy, Antioch University-LA

Reverend Patricia Truman reflects the soulful genre and lyrical prose of the Emerald Isles with a true embrace of her ancestral roots.

— **C. Ann Garrick**
retired educator and member of Sacred Circle Group, facilitated by Rev. Truman

Patty Truman's words flow from her heart and soul. Each poem is an inspiration and a reflection of her sacred journeys, each inviting the reader to glimpse the mystical. Her strong connection to nature and her deep love and respect for Mother Earth are ever present. Reading this poetry will ignite your senses and guide you deeper within, as your own soul journey unfolds. For the past twenty years, it has been a great joy to have championed Patty to continue writing and now publish her first book of poetry.

— **Loma Devine**
international art broker and curator

Patricia takes us on a magical journey of the heart, awakening us with the beauty of her words. She enlivens us with her mystical compendium of life's journey as she leads us into the pathway of the heart. She brings to our lives a true gift of the power of love and healing in her poems that awaken our hearts to the beauty of who we are.

— **Finbarr Ross**
 author of *Sacred Mystical Journey: A Life Journey from Tragedy to Triumph.* www.sacredmysticaljourneys.com

What you hold in your hands is a modern-day mystic's contemplation of the nature of life and your part in it. Searching, deeply moving into the intimate spaces within heart and mind, Patricia Truman leads the way. Sometimes playful but always personal, the poet evokes images of a searcher, a walker through the journey of life, using the theme that the walker determines her own path, exploring the depths and heights and breadths of human consciousness. The book examines the concept that every individual creates their own life, moment by moment, by the choices made. She makes clear that the wanderer's path is sacred, containing portals and passages for each of us to glimpse the mystical. Every chapter focuses on an aspect of life.

From the first page, the reader is invited to see life through the eyes of the Divine. This book of poetry is one to be read slowly and pondered. It is deeply evocative, providing lush images that impel the reader to question assumptions and look more deeply at life. Deeply mystical, it whispers; it doesn't shout. It playfully prods and pokes. This is an exploration of consciousness, asking if there is a divine plan to follow and then answering that it seems so.

Patricia writes:

> For where my little will
> bows to a wiser will
> and my true identity, more clearly
> comes forth,
> and I more easily relax into a larger, wiser
> unnamed prompting from the unseen,
> but deeply felt
>> Eternal Authority.

Walk mindfully and savor this treasure.

— **Rev. Dr. Heather Dawn Clark**
  senior minister, Center for Spiritual Living Capistrano Valley

I have known Patty Truman for forty years, and I have read her poetic writings with amazement. She has a gift. She sits down and writes, and the words just come naturally. This book is not a product of academic instruction but a product of her own style. I am pleased that with its publication, all may enjoy her gifts.

— **John Blick**
  Blick Industries

AUTHOR'S GRATITUDE

I find it difficult to express how touched I am by the glowing and humbling tributes to this collection of poetry to be shared with those of similar mind and heart. In truth, I feel as if I have just been faithful for forty years—to sit in silence, asking for guidance—and somehow pen flows across the page. Thus, I have been encouraged to contribute these gifts as the scribe. A deep intuitive knowing whispered that they were not for me alone but to be shared.

It has been by such encouragement as well as being nudged by the "Divine Elbow" within to bring forth this work even as I hesitated, questioning the next indicated steps. With great gratitude to those teachers, friends, and associates in business and ministry who have so generously shared their acknowledgements, I have continued the journey into print.

Since childhood, I have found joy in using colored pencils to draw pictures in books. I find it enhances my experience and enriches my ownership of a book and its messages. Dear reader, do find delight in doing the same if it brings you joy.

May Mystic Cloud Walker's words touch, heal, expand, inspire, or perhaps delight you. This is my deepest soul prayer.

Patricia Truman

FOREWORD

At its best, poetry is the expression of spirit in dialogue with the great mysteries. Poetry parts the veils and establishes identity, creating community as it does so. Poetry heals the wounded, the confused, the lost. And the poet is a healer.

Not all poetry rises to this level, of course, yet the poetry we remember and value most always does. Rev. Patricia Truman's poetry consistently gifts the reader with such experience. As a poet, Truman channels a divine light. She is a gifted witness, an empathic traveler who walks with us in our footsteps.

> Once I was a Woman Wild
> A woman free of spirit and heart.
> Once I ran with the beauty of wolves.
> Once with all Earth I was a part—

In this poem and others collected here, Truman writes memorably about what it means to be a woman and a human being searching for and embodying faith in a confusing, often divisive and threatening world. One of her many gifts as a poet is that she rises above the topical to express profound insights and wisdom. Often, the poetry rises to the expression of a Seer—for what is the prophetic poet if not a Seer?

Truman's strong roots ascend from ancient traditions and civilizations. This is the poetry of a world traveler, a curious historian, an archaeologist, and a student of time itself, a poetry in which the rebellious and the cloistered find clarity and voice.

It is also poetry immersed in the beauty, mystery, and timelessness of the natural world, a voice that a naturalist like John Muir would recognize and admire. It is familiar with the elements and the storms and calms that toss and confuse the human heart. In fact, Truman's free rhythms and poems in traditional forms closely align with the measure of the heart, which science has now been able to map.

Most of all, though, this poet is a healer and desirable companion. Following and describing the arc of a long, active life, her poems create hope and provide comfort for those who travel with them. They are steady and right companions in any emotional weather. They instruct, commiserate, woo, entice, celebrate, and offer warm embrace. Is that not poetry's highest calling?

Reading Patricia Truman's poems helps me reassess and redirect my own spiritual and physical journey in this realm. If you are fortunate enough to discover this book, may it be so with you.

— Robert McDowell
Poet, speaker, social activist for the advancement of women's rights, educator, and author of sixteen books, including *Poetry as a Spiritual Practice* and *The World Next to This One*

DEDICATION

This collection of musings, poetry, and amplifications I humbly dedicate to my teachers along this Earth Walk. Some are present and others nonphysical.

In the beginning, parents are our first teachers. Mine were Wesley Webb and Elizabeth Reilly Peper. My dear mother instilled in me proper manners and grammar and imparted a portion of her graciousness, for which I am ever grateful. My father opened my mind to metaphysics, curiosity, and a dedication to being healthy, since he was in ill health for most of my life.

My three children—Kern Dunagan, Jennifer Dunagan Jackson, and Laural Truman Taylor—have been profound teachers on many levels. In motherhood and as grownups, they have shown me how to be an adult friend to them.

The proud experience of gazing at one's newborn babe bursts the heart open in a way no other does, love fragmenting us into thousands of caring pieces. As they grew from childhood into adulthood, my children were my instructors who taught me how to maneuver through the many lessons they would teach me on my own life's journey, including tolerance, forgiveness, and love. The magnitude of Divine Love and compassion and how it transcended our difficulties seared into my being. Along with the power of prayer, I was shown life-changing miracles. Each one of my children, so different from the other, were my guides. I do believe children come to refine our souls.

Life, travel, friends, and varied experiences each brought forth a part hidden within me to be discovered, uncovered, and explored. Experiencing love, betrayal, disappointment, and heartbreaking or delightful times forces us to go deep within to discover parts of ourselves we never knew existed.

This is where I realized I had been enrolled in "Life School," and the curriculum was for soul expansion.

As I grew, teachers, friends, and family touched me in various ways, all adding to the rich coloration of my life. My professional life, sacred and ministerial studies and ordination, helped mold me into who I am. Life offered me so much more with marriages, loving relationships, each opening my heart even further to experience the joy and tears of life.

In my travels, each land on which I placed my feet had a concept or precept that deepened my realization of the oneness of all humanity. The Earth itself has given a marvelous revelatory understanding of various people, customs, traditions, beauty, creativity, and living skills. Since childhood, nature has sweetly taught me in mystical nonverbal lessons, examples, and beauty that swelled my heart into welcome newness.

The Divine Presence being sensed since early childhood has always been the constant sustaining force in my life. Angels, guides, spirit, inner voice, intuition, and what I call the "Divine Elbow"— a thousand expressions of the unity of all creation are still my companions, unseen and unheard but dearly known and felt each and every day.

Glimpses of my life portrayed in this small volume, originally written for our now enlarging family—currently ten grandchildren and twenty-one great grandchildren—keeps me learning, growing, and stretching to be the best me I can be.

Sincere gratitude to everyone
who has ever contributed to my unfolding
Pilgrim Path,

Patricia Truman

TABLE OF CONTENTS

Author's Gratitude . . . . *x*

Foreword . . . . *xi*

Dedication . . . . *xiii*

      A Tribute to Antonio Machado *1*

      A Poet's Reflection on Antonio Machado's Poem . . . *2*

Chapter 1 — FOOTPRINTS ON THE SANDS OF TIME

      Wanderer, Your Footsteps Are the Path *5*

      Who Is the Author? *6*

      Mystic Cloud Walker *7*

      Mystic Walking *10*

      Wild Woman *12*

      1000 Angel Faces *15*

      Magic Is Everywhere! *16*

      My Faithful Feet Friends *18*

      The Sea and She *19*

      Feet In the Sand *20*

      The Pathway *23*

      Pausing *25*

      The Wonder of Wondering *26*

      Footprints of Friendships *27*

      Roses In the Lemon Tree *29*

      The Red Dusty Road *30*

Chapter 2 — EARTH WALKING

      Walker, There Is No Road *33*

      Bare Feet *34*

      The Mode of Transportation
          for Our Earth *36*

      Dance of Hope for the Universe *39*

      All the Same Beneath the Skin *41*

      I Know Who You Are *43*

Darkness 45
Distinction 46
Rain, A Metaphor for Tears 48
For the Youths In My Life 50
All the Wee Children 51
Identity and Will 52
Cinderella Imprint 54

Chapter 3 — THE SACRED PATH
Walker, Traveler, Pilgrim—
Walking Creates the Road 57

On the Sacred Path 58
Pilgrim Walk 59
The Voice 61
Song of the Ancients 62
The Unfolding 66
Dancing Feet 68
Rain Walking 70
Journeys, Pilgrimages, Passages
        of Seasons 71
Wandering 74
Generational Curse 76
Inner Road to Outer Path 79

Chapter 4 — SOLE TO SOUL
One Unrepeatable Step at a Time 83

Soul Journey 84
Come Away, My Lovely 85
Embracing the Mystery 88
The Labyrinth 89
In the Kingdom of Divine Love,
        There Is No Chastisement 92
Glory 94
A Walk Celebrating Agelessness 95

Releasing and Allowing 98
The Walk of a Thousand Veils 100
Fingers In the Dirt 101
Sunday Morning Silence 102
I Dance On the Edge of Your Dreams 104

Chapter 5 — PORTALS AND PASSAGES

Foam Trails Upon the Sea, Then Gone 107

Portal 108
Birthing Portal 109
Mystical Portals 111
Ode to Painting — "Monastery of Olde" 113
Naked I Stand 114
Dare to Stand Naked 115
Beyond Mystical Portal 117
A Naked Raw Prayer 119
Turn Sideways Into the Light 120
Passages Into a New Phase of Life 122
Passage 124
What New Doorway Beckons 126
Steps to Understand Life Path 127
My Mind Flutters — The Dream 129
Ireland 131
Travel 133

Chapter 6 — REFLECTIONS OF JOURNEY

*The Path Has Made the Road —
There Is No Other Way* 135

I Am Thousands of Women 136
Light 138
Reflections Regarding
        Standing Stone — Aging 139
Ancient Bubbles from the
        Pond of Remembrance 141

The Great Pond of Life 142

Empty 144

Half-Used Bed 146

Frame and Re-Frame 147

New Path 148

Life Is a River Raft 150

The River of Life 152

Deepest Self Singing the Song
    of One's Being 154

One Unobserved Step at a Time 156

New Moon 158

Chapter 7 — THE JOURNEY WANES

A Road Never To Be Trod Again 161

The Hourglass 162

Breath 163

Grateful Heart 164

The House of Silence —
    The Pandemic 2020 - 2021 166

Yin Arising Women 168

My Only Son 170

Friends' Farewell 171

One So Small World 173

Veil Parts 175

I Am One With All That Is 177

Death — Disappearance 179

Death and Awakening 180

Footprints 181

Dear Ones Rejoice — A Farewell Poem 183

Birthing of a Book 184

Artists' Acknowledgements 185

About The Author 188

MYSTIC CLOUD WALKER

earth walk

A TRIBUTE
TO ANTONIO MACHADO

WANDERER

Wanderer, your footsteps are
the road, and nothing more.
Wanderer, there is no road.
The road is made by walking.
By walking, one makes the road,
and upon glancing behind,
one sees the path
that never will be trod again.
Wanderer, there is no road —
only wakes upon the sea.

— BY ANTONIO MACHADO

A POET'S REFLECTION ON ANTONIO MACHADO'S POEM

Your road is made by walking.
There is no other way.

Being mindful of the inner prompts
And outer signposts,
one finds their way, a step at a time.
One day, one moment,
a breath—inhale, exhale
until looking over your shoulder
seeing the path where one's footstep
shall never fall again.
What lies behind is the past.
What lies ahead, revealed by,
embraced by the seductive mystery.
A destiny created by walking
seems there is no other way.

Things too heavy or cumbersome
for the journey are discarded
along the way.
First, the lesser important baggage
in a moment.
Eventually, the hidden things surface
beginning to irritate reluctantly, are deemed
too detrimental to carry
any longer.

Affecting health or well-being,
walker chooses the higher road
allowing one's long-embedded habits,
ways of maneuvering to fall away,
lightening the journey
freed from the cumbersome
rituals, habits, denials,
a new wind blows, the road opens
into territories of possibilities
not yet seen or offered before.
The road is made by
walking, listening, responding
taking the path calling forth
the next indicated step, thus so it goes,
there is no other way.

Wanderer, traveler, pilgrim
there is no road.
Your road is created by walking
your own way.

CHAPTER 1

FOOTPRINTS ON THE SANDS OF TIME

Wanderer, Your Footsteps Are The Path

WHO IS THE AUTHOR?

If I am the author of my life
     what story do I want to write?
What chapters do I wish to edit
     reframing the situation or drama?
What color do I wish to paint in the lines?
     What is the name of my book?

If I am the author, whose voice do I use?
     Is it a conversation, a narrative, poetry or prose?
What language suits my voice?
     Is there a plot or reflective memoir?
What chapters am I now placing
in my book?

I choose the writing materials, the look.
     I am editor-in-chief and humble recipient.
I am the star and the unseen presence.
     I am creator and the created,
every chapter by my hand writ
     in this mystical book.

MYSTIC CLOUD WALKER

When she was a child
she trod Earth's dusty path
      dragging a stick behind
            to leave her mark.

When she was a little older
she loved to look upon her footprints in the sand
      and then sadly see the tide, like waves of time
          wash them away.

As a teen, she participated,
sang, danced and dated,
      leaving her lipstick mark
         on the passing parade.

As a young mother
she knew there had been a mark
      made in time
         on the lives of her children.

So diverse, so interesting
wholly their own
      and yet
         her.

As she matured,
she made a mark
      on business for some years.
         She was known and recognized.

She left a mark
on good works in the local scene —
        the youth club, the college
                experienced her loving energy.

As the days drifted by
the young girl
        who once attached strings to drifting clouds,
                walking them as favorite pets

now walked
among the clouds,
        her vision blurred
                by cares and concerns.

Yet
one day,
        she will again be
                the Mystic Cloud Walker.

But no cloud tethered
by a string,
        but she herself
                will walk upon the clouds.

As once she flew
through the clouds
        in a great silver bird
                taking her

from country to country,
exotic
and mystical places,

she will soon
transcend the need of silver bird,
and walk barefoot across
the billowing expanse

of the heavens,
leaving footprints
on the cloudy horizon.

Mystic Cloud Walker,
mystical lady, mother, lover, friend,
purveyor of personal dreams,
poet ...

Mystic Cloud Walker
walks into the haze
beyond the horizon,
still quietly leaving her mark

like a small stick
being pulled down
a dusty trail.
Mystic Cloud Walker, one day, a farewell

MYSTIC WALKING

The Mystic Cloud Walker finds her way
through the rubble of modern life
placing carefully, a perfectly manicured foot
walking the path of peace not strife.

Taking barbs without retort
praying for those with sharpened tongue,
turning a cheek, appearing weak.
Yet in Spirit's strength, work is done.

The unseen hand guides her journey
tho unseen looking on her behalf
calming the water that could upset
separating the wheat meat from shaft,
Mystic Cloud Walker

Appearing remote yet passionately alive deep within
praying and thinking in another realm
detached appearance yet ethereal grin.
Who can know her?
They only think they do
acquaintances,
many and varied,
but close to her, few.

The Mystic Cloud Walker
must have time alone
to dream, not cluttered
with things.

It is her life blood and air
Mystic Cloud Walker,
not what she sees.
Mystic, mystic walking with your cloud
On a string.

WILD WOMAN

Once I was a Woman Wild
A woman free of spirit and heart.
Once I ran with the beauty of wolves.
Once with all Earth I was a part —

A part of all that God had made
Glorious life, I was unafraid.
Then you entered with charm and fun
That was the beginning of me undone.

The first tether was to the bed,
A silk gossamer line, I was wed.
You placed it gently around my waist
So thin I hardly noticed changing pace.

Then came a tether to stove and home.
This was my duty, no longer to roam,
Clipped were the wings soaring with eagle gold,
Now I was being "suggested" and unkindly told.

Then came the rope to cradle dear,
A love unlike any did in me sear —
Into my fiber and bone,
My life now under a crystal dome.

Over the years, more tethers came.
So many I cannot all of them name —
Security, financial and tribe,
A new way owned me; I did subscribe.

The charm and fun, where did they go?
I had forgotten all that I know.
Wild Woman numb by tethers she chose,
Wild Woman captive from inner "no's."

One day, the cradle empty for years,
That child now grown, farewell with tears.
Something inside had stirred anew...
Is it the me that used to be you?
The smell on the air calls inner me.
Can I remember the invisible see?
My teeth now dull cannot seem to cut
Through tethers that hold me in a rut.

But desire for mountaintops
Trees, streams, and no stops
Burns within me, I cannot put it out.
The flame burns my tethers all about.

First, I am free from the lure of things.
My heart for truth within me springs.
Then the hearth and home dull in view,
I know my truth will survive even you.

Slowly they fall from waist and hand,
The Wild Woman will surely stand.
The golden hair now mixed with gray
But of the spirit, what will it say?

I AM ME! I long to run with wolves
Like a doe up the mountain on cloven hoof.
No longer the pain of cutting word
I'm free at last like a glorious bird.

Free at last, free at last.
Here is the new. Gone is the past.
Free to be the best I can be,
And wondrous thing, I'll be truly me!

1000 ANGEL FACES

The Mystic Cloud Walker walks the sky at night.
Unseen by even herself or others
She travels to galaxies far flung,
Conversing with sisters and brothers.

The Mystic Cloud Walker walks upon the clouds
Voluminous PUFFY whites traveling the sky.
She relishes in the ability to be in both worlds,
One in the daytime, other at night, a fantasy fly.

Fantasy in physical but reality in soul
For she is escorted by many who instruct,
The things she of her own accord
Could never really learn, a soul level reconstruct.

Mystic Cloud Walker, you love to gaze
At clouds silently drifting by.
You look and see shapes and visions
That delight your wandering eye.

Mystic Cloud Walker, you are aptly named
For you are an eager learner and adventurous, too.
We welcome you nightly to your cloud romp
And always there is purpose; teachers come to you.

Go on your way this day,
Mystic Cloud Walker, hidden from sight.
Go about your practical ways and work
And we will see you again tonight!

Go and be blessed and bless.

MAGIC IS EVERYWHERE!

Being ready for magic is a wondrous thing
        yes, there is magic!
The sun each faithful morning,
        the sea churning, creating atmosphere
just right for our living on this lovely planet.
        Eternally in you, the true You has existed,
will exist, not dependent upon time or locale.
        Eternal energy means every living thing partaking
        of life either
on this plane or elsewhere in the cosmology of
        the higher realms, never dies, only changes.

Only faintly known to morals encapsulated within the
        confines of an earthly body-mind
there is a heart-mind that exists in the onward journey
        as an individual soul expression,
until each soul advances to the unity of oneness with the
        one infinite source of love, life, creation and
all that has ever been or will be.
        That is magic in the making, moment by moment,
breath by breath, thought by thought.
        Yes, expect magic!
        Be aware of magic!
See magic everywhere in nature's green and growing
        concerto of every imaginable shape, shade, fruit, nut
        grain, leaf, and flower.

Surely the growth from seed to food is magic!
    Green grass chewed by animals becomes
    eatable protein.
The world's diversity is amazingly magical,
    bird songs, wind in the pines, rustle of palm trees,
    melodies everywhere.
Music in the mind of a composer or musician resulting
    in magical notes, songs, concertos, operas and more
    touching hearts and minds.
The trained dedicated body of a dancer expresses magic
    in various styles and movements.
The talented hands of artists listening to their inward muse
    expressing in numerous forms, structures,
    pictorials, canvas,
    walls, ceilings, clay, wood, cloth, earth, and stone.
Written words dancing into aliveness from the writer onto
    page producing literature—stories, dramas, prose,
    film, poetry,
magic from thought to expression.

The many moving parts of creativity from teacher to students,
    parent to child, mentor to learner, institutions
    to stimulate
and inspire shaping whole cultures.
    Magic is holy and sacred and resides within each of us.
Magic is absolutely everywhere,
    allowing vibrant magic to be a part of this
    very moment!

MY FAITHFUL FEET FRIENDS

My feet have walked on desert sand,
Grass green, pavement sizzling hot,
Icy snow, cement cities, cobblestone lanes.
        Dear feet, you are my faithful friends.

How many dirt and sand strewn lands —
Israel oasis, Mexican shores, Sinai, Red Sea
Beaches, jungle, mud around the world.
        Lovely dusty faithful feet friends.

Waterfalls, swimming in mountain streams,
Rocks, boulders, like a gazelle, a child skipping.
High Sierras, Yosemite, Golan Heights, Himalayas,
        Fearless faithful feet friends.

North America, Ethiopia, Kenya, Tanzania,
Uganda, South Africa, Egypt now looms large.
What terrain awaits my traveling path ahead,
        Exploring faithful feet friends?

Today my feet tingle with anticipation, trepidation
Aliveness reminiscent of fire walk and marathon,
More alive, new kind of sensitivity and awareness
        Holy anointed faithful feet friends.

THE SEA AND SHE

Like many before her and
Those numerous ones to follow
She loves to walk by the sea.

Many shores have felt her foot bare
Leaving an imprint of her presence
Soon to be washed away — being is key.

Mexico, Bali, Israel, Alaska
California, New York, Florida, Texas
China, Brazil, Ireland, Greece ... ecstasy.

All have touched her soul and soles,
Sea speaking in voiceless ceaseless charm
Sometimes angry, rough or playful and free.

Many are called to mountain majesty,
Others to vast deserts' silent spaciousness
Rivers' roar or valleys' quiet; some come to the sea.

Singing its song of coming and going
Beckoning, receding, teasing, embracing
Warm, cold, moody, sweet; no repeat.

Sun rises, she and sea reimagined, unpredictable,
Colors of every shade appearing, disappearing,
Depths affront her shallow pools inviting to see.

Like many dreamers she loves the sea —
Beautiful solace, sanctuary, friend, confidant
No image, pretense, duty; a repose to just be.

Yes, the years have come and the years do go,
    yet the ocean keeps washing upon the shore.
What invisible hand draws the line that holds back the sea?
    What intelligence allows it to come this close,
    but no more?

What invisible presence guides our lives and fate?
    How much input do we have into cosmic eternity?
When I walk by the sea in quiet contemplation of the "All in All,"
    I sense a unity of the oneness of sky, sand, sea and me.

Somehow, I seem to know that which I find, this space,
    this connectedness with all that I see,
then I have some input into the events of my life
    for in that unison of love comes inner harmony.
Yes, I am grateful for this day to walk by the sea,
    to live so close and take the time to refresh
remembering the days there were and looking forward
    to the days that are still to come, placing my mind at rest.

An afterthought —
I look forward with anticipation to a day at the beach with each
of my beloveds.
A lazy day of gentle talk, swimming, reading, thinking,
and being.
A day to just enjoy being in Laguna, relishing the gift and
beauty it is.
Strolling for many miles with no appointment to keep.

The children were young like little dolphins in the water from morning to night.
I too was young.
A rare day, a precious day, one that I hope to soon repeat enjoying with expanded family,
not the same of course, but taking time to honor my life today,
accepting just as it is and just as it is not.

THE PATHWAY

Divine Love with whom I am One
 To Whom I say, "Good morning, unknown yet
 knowing Divine."
Many posture as to their knowledge
 Yet I know we do not know fully.
We only glimpse through the veil darkly.

My mind is crowded with facts of God,
 My very vocabulary spews memorized words starkly.
My reactions are appropriate to the rituals of this age
 Yet rituals are only dances without music emanating
 from within.

All peoples express Spirit through the filter of their own
cultural exposure
 Calling this force forth by thousands of names in
 every conceivable language.
  I know I do not truly know the breadth and
  depth of the infinite,
   And yet am in the diligent process
   of knowing.

My heart senses a deep truth whispered to me in silence,
 My intuition responds to a wisdom just beyond the
 edge of my light.
  The unifying power of silence leads me
  beyond words
   Enriching me more deeply in
   mystical ways.

Every cell and molecule of my amazing lovingly
created vehicle
 Seems to know how to breathe, assimilate, ingest,
 digest, eliminate.

Also, how to help, heal and speak if I will
but listen
> In the silence is where I have learned
> to hear.

There is a knowing within me that requires great solitude
and quiet to hear
> When involved in a task, then the Holy does ask,
> "Have you thought of this?"
>> Revelatory streams rush into the arid desert
>> of my parched soul —

I am refreshed
I am enlivened
I am knowing at a level that is deeper than sound
I am sensing beyond feeling
I am receiving through each cell and molecule
in my being
> They are my receptors, receptive to the
> great unknown
>> Yet being known presence.

How marvelous, how humbling, how divine the silence,
> Enabled to enter into a fuller consciousness and
> brighter light.
>> Humbled by this gift, so I shall always be
>> a silent receiver,
>>> For the revelation of the unseen
>>> but felt.

Refining this instrument within my mind gifts of deeper
perceptions of truth.
> With great gratitude thankfulness moves
> me to a place
>> Of expanded illumination and sweet
>> connection.

PAUSING

There are some times I love,
    absolutely love
        to do nothing

but sit in the sun
    and stare at
        my flowers bursting with beauty

observing the breeze
    gently teaching
        the leaves to dance.

feeling the sun
    warm my awaiting skin,
        having spent too much time
            on computer and phone.

And oh, to listen
    no human sound
        answering no questions
            holding no positions.

Allowing bird songs to
    lift my heart
        soothe my soul
            delight my senses.

This is one of the
    sacred acts
        of care for my soul,
            doing absolutely nothing.

THE WONDER OF WONDERING

There is a great merit in wondering,
questioning and finding one's own answer.
There is great mental stimulus in wondering,
discovering for my soul truth that romances.

Romances the beauty and nobility of life
creating a system of belief that is comfortable,
making friends with the inconsistencies of life
and finding in chaos, some order dependable.

I suppose this is faith or fate of some sort
not in an image, object, or person outside
but finding truth that resounds within my soul,
harmonious, not answers that constantly chide.

Answers that cause guilt and shame,
reasons that justify hate and vengeance, tyranny.
These thought patterns do not fare well for me,
a deeper inquiry of wonder embraces the mystery.

There is a wonder in wondering and challenging the norm.
It is pleasant to have thoughts that come from realms unseen
accessing eternal wisdom from ages gone and to come
carrying a treasure of small gold nuggets mined in pondering.

Wonder, Mystic Cloud Walker.
Explore the heavens as high as you can go.
Wonder the depths, the width, the heights
for your own peace of mind, the inner know.

This is where the jewels are found
exploring books of diversity and challenge.
Not all fit or are accepted, but within the search,
that vein of gold is found again and again,
bit by bit the treasure chest is filled to my soul's delight.

FOOTPRINTS OF FRIENDSHIP

Each individualized soul that appears in my life
        for a moment, months, many years, or eons,
leaves an imprint pressed upon my heart and mind.

New little family grands and great grands
        entering, expanding the life experiences,
each one carrying its own relationship touch.

Some seem like old souls reentering our world
        bringing needed light, laughter, wisdom, love
a gift not fully opened, unfolding day by day.

Each sweet little soul arriving like an invitation
        to our own vulnerability
humbly witnessing a new generation's innate intuition.

Carrying invisible help as a natural way of discernment
        observing, listening, and, alas, copying adults,
but also retaining their own innate ground of being.

Strangers in a new land full of curiosity and joy
        being shaped by the place they are raised,
carrying the silent soul, vows made before entering.

Thus, we observe, endeavor to enrich, shepherd,
        yet the spring within them is hidden in winter
to be revealed as their own awakening unfolds.

The intimacy of incarnation nudging us all
to find that path for which our foot was designed,
our steps do count imprinting upon the human story of life.

May each step be carefully taken, mindfully
leaving a pathway behind us revealing our essence;
we all have a vibrational imprint upon the collective
consciousness.

ROSES IN THE LEMON TREE

There she stood,
    straggly yet noble with her golden lemon orbs
intertwined among her thorny old branches
    climbing a rose bush blooming.
Was this not the perfect metaphor for life?

Roses in the Lemon Tree
    came from the fertile mind of my mother
for a book that was trapped within her
    and never written,
yet still wanting to come forth into being.

Many years ago, the inner muse
    arose within me, bringing poetry
to my amazement and humbling delight.
    The pen on white paper, a love affair
that has now long persisted.

Desiring to share some of my journey
    vicissitudes of life
for my ever-increasing family,
    hopeful some wisdom will come
facilitating journeys of those called to partake.

What stories to tell? How many journeys to reveal?
    Which lessons learned living experiences?
The writing will reveal what wants to come forth.
    Being faithful to show up to the page, following my heart,
the unfolding journey began long ago and so continues.

THE RED DUSTY ROAD

The red road has many terrains.
Some days, the dust is thick and red.
Others, the ooze from rains is slime;
hot days, the earth is hard as lead.

Seasons come and then fade away
leaving traces of what has been.
Still, I walk unceasingly, persistently,
journeying to where I did first begin.

Is the red road really a hoop?
Traveling by white moon and black rain
thinking there is a destination ahead,
yet at the end returning as I began.

The everlasting hoop of life
eternity fashioned in pictorial form.
The carvings left inscribed day by day
telling the journey from where we were born.

Like the red road when rains have come,
imprints captured deep by the red clay
so each word, action, thought and deed
on life's hoop are etched, even to this day.

As we travel the dusty red road
sing your own special song loud and clear.
Dance your dance to the drumbeat within.
Chant, pray, grow and learn, each step, hold dear.

The long red road stretching,
circular is our soul journey loop
swirling and twirling Earth spinning.
We are all in the divine sacred hoop.

May we all walk well, my brothers and sisters.
Walk well.

CHAPTER 2

EARTH
WALKING

Walker, There Is No Road

BARE FEET

Fundamental to life
is standing in the dirt.
Babies are born, cherished, cleaned
when able to crawl or waddle,
head for the dirt.

Earth, Mother Earth, her bare breast
exposed, miles of barren soil
then adorned with greens
of unimaginable shades and textures,
sprouting wildflowers, meadows, forests
jungles, deserts, and glens.

Moss, ancient like delicate lace
abutting tropical leafy vibrant display,
shocks of red, pink, and most always
a vibrant touch of yellow.
She is a naked woman at times,
also, a queen attired royally.

Dirt, dirty, lusty fungal dirt, elemental soil
from which life in countless forms springs,
Everything needed for the sustenance,
survival of all life on this planet
comes from her giving, birthing womb,
ever fertile, passionate abundance.

Everything humankind has arrives in raw form,
birthed from her endless creative bounty.
Bare hands and feet touching sacred earth

sense a connection to something
transcendent, primal, ancient,
present and immensely holy.

Children intuitively know this.
They play in the dirt, make mud pies
taste it, not feeling dirty at all.
Mud squishing between toes
a sensual delight, one with the source
of all things.

Mud fights, mud baths and facials,
hands embracing a clump of clay
return one to what has always been
humbling, balancing yin and yang,
speaking some prehistoric message
to which tactile cells respond.

Appreciating my faithful feet
prodding many lands of sand
dirt, stone, which is petrified soil,
loom, farms, jungles, mulch-covered ground
fertile lands, arid sands, red clay, sandy beaches
and dusty African plains.

My feet have loved it all,
filthy, unkempt, happy traveling feet.
One thing they still long to trod,
red grapes crushed beneath their sole
into wine, red robust warmed by Tuscan sun ...
ah, one day her bounty staining my bare feet.

THE MODE OF TRANSPORTATION
FOR OUR EARTH

Feet, feet, wonderful feet take every step, every day where
we choose to go.
A few attributes of our amazingly wonderful feet:
dance
trot
run
work
play
hold us upright
need rest at night
take us on great travels
stay at home
pedal
swim
like mud squishing between their toes
splash in streams, oceans, creeks, lakes and rivers
ski
play ball
race
need rubbing, care and pedicures
are pretty, ordinary and not so attractive
feet like to be touched
tap
keep time to music
stomp
caress
play footsie

kick
nudge
open stuck doors
dance on their toes
point
leave footprints
silent
loud
stomp
tiptoe
sneak
announce themselves
climb
walk on wire
walk on rope
balance
support our bodies
are our companions
get amputated
lose part of themselves and still function
grow callous
bunions
ache
fallen arches
flat footed
light footed
heavy footed
dainty
hairy
big
little

soft
harsh
climb
help braid rope
have 10 toes normally
come in all sizes and colors
big foot
webbed
and probably many more wonderful functions.

Feet, dear precious feet—how many stored memories, expressions and experiences have we shared?

I love my feet, where they have taken me, supported me, helped me explore ancient sites, many kinds of terrains, climates, earth's expression in forests, jungles, deserts, cities, towns, villages, beaches, waters, and so much more.

I hope this little book allows you to fall deeply in love with your feet, then your whole body and all its wonders, warts, imperfections, and beauty.

Hands—think about hands as your tools of life. Our unseen parts functioning by divine wisdom and design.

Infinite Impulse within every part of our magnificent bodies to heal themselves if supported and cared for; fed with nourishing, healthy foods, pure water, and positive, kind, loving thoughts of oneself and all others.

Loving ourselves—body, mind, heart, soul and spirit—this is true power.

DANCE OF HOPE FOR THE UNIVERSE

God and Mother Nature did a dance
created a planet full of many plants
thinking it was such fun,
they danced until it was done.

All creation abundantly adorned
trees, plants, fruits, even vine of thorn.
They danced and danced
into a beautiful trance.

Creating verdant magnificence
covering the earth with luscious scents
they danced and danced,
united in love, whirling and twirling.

And still today dancing two
each morning, fresh and new
escorting summer, spring and fall,
introducing winter snow and all.

Dancing through universe
singing each eon, a new verse
ever changing, expanding in scope
filling the universe with never-ending hope.

We, like a fiddler on the roof,
keeping our footing secure
while balancing many balls in the air,

participating in life graciously
and not being a fool.

What skills are required to live —
householder, cook, creator, gardener
teacher, student, spouse, parent, lover
and not fail at any?

Young, vibrant, sexual, intellectual,
empathetic, strong, vulnerable,
teachable, pliable, resilient, steady,
endeavor not to break apart.
Ah...humans are marvelous,
innovative, brave, scared, confused,
sinners, saints, pacifists, warriors
being sometimes all at once.

Living, laughing, loving,
hating, angry, remorseful, forgiving,
young, middle-aged, elder, ancient,
doing all with measured grace.

Life is like the fiddler on the roof
making your best music
while walking the narrow roof ridge
playing and not falling.

To daughters and son, grands, and great grands
in my Tribe

ALL THE SAME BENEATH THE SKIN

She is near the age of granddaughters.
She is beautifully black with scarification,
signature of beauty for her.
They are pretty, white, and secretly
getting tattoos out of sight.
She is proud of her breasts and enlarged ears.
They, proud of their breasts and pierced ears,
each displaying in different ways.

Black girls do the hard work of the village.
Children, carrying wood, farming, cooking,
and ceremoniously being beaten.
White girls looking for ease, luxury,
asking for help with children, cooking,
and carrying wood, usually divorce
if they are beaten.

Beneath the skin, they want the same things —
a good life, a loving man and future.
Western media mindsets, African tribal mindsets,
each moving forward in their own way.

Ethiopian women walk barefoot in the dirt with callouses.

California girls wear pretty sandals with painted toenails.

Black girls have one or two garments, some beaded jewelry.

White girls have too many clothes and lots of junk jewelry

They live in different worlds but want the same things —

a good life, a loving husband, beautiful healthy children,

good food and loving families.

In truth, we are all the same beneath the skin

each obtaining in our own way.

I KNOW WHO YOU ARE

I know who you are.
>You are the one nursing the babies,
>>sitting up all night with sick ones.

I know who you are.
>You are the supportive, dependable,
>>ever-encouraging unseen partner
>>>while he is out, about, basking in glory.

I know who you are.
>You are the one who sees that all are dressed well,
>>and you will get a new outfit next time.

I know who you are.
>You see your sons, husbands, brothers, and friends
>>go off to war
>>>while you hold down the home front —
>>>>jobs, family, farm, business,
>>>>children,
>>>>>church and community.
>When they return maimed and manic
>>you nurse, hold, help and love.

I know who you are.
>You are tired and weary
>>of building others' lives
>>>while yours disappears.

I know who you are,
    feeling now is your time
        to find the authentic you who was lost
           in the rush of doing riot
               of living others' lives —
                   family, friend, client,
                   church,
                   corporations and financial needs.

I know who you are.
    You want a conversation
        at long last about you.
           Where do I go from here?
             Who am I really?
               What do I want?
             What? When? How? Who?

Weeping alone, who to care?
    Gut wrenching loneliness, who to share?
        Pain unseen seems so unfair.
           Break me open, do I care?

Encapsulated in frozen emotion
    numb from years of nonrecognition.
        Something stirring, wanting resurrection,
           awaken from the dead, a faint
           recollection.

No matter the story and lie,
    awaken from the trance we buy.
        Step into your own insistent why,
           a vibration that will not die.

DARKNESS

Darkness since childhood
      has not been my friend;
things unseen, have frightened,
      anxiously awaiting the return of light.

It seems most frightening occurrences
      happen in the dark.
The manifestation of tragedy
      comes from darkened places in mind or heart.

Those drawn to the light carry brightness.
      Darkness always hated the light
endeavoring in human history
      to snuff out radiance too bright to endure.

Light dispels darkness.
      That which is done in the dark
shall be and is revealed in light.
      Light, light shine on us brightly,
         filling, enveloping,
            holding us.

                    Light, Light, Holy Light —

DISTINCTION

One goes forth each day.
The sands of time shifting,
one breath and exhale
until the last breath
        leaving a space distinctive.

Each thing that takes life —
an animal, a plant, or human ...
days are marked by actions taken
        each life, each distinction.

So, go this day with awareness
of the gift of life, breath, and choice
for this will never be again.
Quietly or publicly, what we do
        leaves a mark distinctive.

Is it the prayers said awakening?
The intention to be relevant?
Choices, many or few selected
create the movement, the action
        giving life direction.

The books we read or not,
the poems savored, memorized or not,
the opportunities to learn, grow or not
create a pattern of being relevant
        or with little distinction.
The Creator did not do it to you.
Opportunities and choices abound.

Self-inflicted limitations and blinders,
a whole-hearted "Yes, let me know!"
        creates full and bright distinction.

No one comes without ability
be it humble or executed well.
That life lived with integrity
faithful doing one's best each day,
        unseen becomes truly distinctive.

For there are eyes that observe
every deed done in private or exposed,
a knower that resided within
speaking clearly
        judging our own distinction.

All are seen, all are known.
All have value not of this plane
All have been a good idea from infinity
How we choose to use our gifts
        create our own distinction.

Self-responsibility is the work.
Our occupations only expose our choices.
How we have chosen to show up in the world
reflects in everything we say or do,
        kind or cruel, integral distinction.

Our lives like our fingerprints
tell who we are clearly,
no two alike, no carbon copies.
Volition is the spiritual gift.
        How used, declares each individualized distinction.

RAIN, A METAPHOR FOR TEARS

Rain, rain that wets the earth
    with heavy fluid,
        the accumulated tears of
            many breaking hearts
                gathered in the spheres
                    and released onto
                        each arid soul.
To metaphorically bring
    new growth,
        new sweet perfume of flowers
            which will come into being
                because of that moisture,
                    that dew which
                        does the
                        miraculous.
Never hide your tears
    or cap them off.
        Allow them to flow
            for the irrigation of
                your inner soul causes
                    and the planetary rain
                    that can bring
                    new life into
                    expression.

In the economy of eternity,

    nothing is lost or wasted.

        All is noticed.

            All is energy on its journey

                to transformation.

Embrace the emotions

    that can bring forth the tears,

        for in that watery offering

            is life, and

                that, more abundantly.

FOR THE YOUTHS IN MY LIFE

Oh, the weight upon the soul for a beloved youth
who takes upon themselves to step off the path,
the sorrow in my heart knowing the fork in the road;
one choice will bring heartache, the other a laugh.

So young to rebel and withdraw
to challenge the ways that are bright,
yet what words can be said to arrest his walk,
what actions to help him choose aright?

Oh, so many times I have laid awake
praying for straying children and kin,
feeling inadequate for the task of parenting.
Is it the base nature that religion calls sin?

Why should they drift from a home with much love?
Why should they seek ways that are disabilities?
My heart aches to know the words to utter
that could touch hearts and realign possibilities.

Where, when is the rainbow?

ALL THE WEE CHILDREN

All the wee children
    of the world
are completely
    themselves
before they are layered
    with shoulds and woulds
dogma and doctrine
    tribal hatred dripping
      with revenge.

Before greed is taught
    as a virtue
and killing as
    honorable
all the small children
    are purely themselves
true to themselves
      in a holy way.

May we learn
    to return to the authentic self
and once more
    be true.

IDENTITY AND WILL

The sternness of willpower is the
engine that drives the life —
a rebellious child exerting his will,
the little foot stomping in timid
                    self-authority

From where does this directiveness arise?
Little mind clearly knowing what it wants
and what does not feel right,
finding personal power in "no" or "yes, I will!"
                    self-authority

The will also helps create identity.
The choices we make shape the life.
The yes's and no's and even the "no decisions" are choices
and color
the portrait we are painting of ourselves.
                    self-authority

How many regrets of yes when I could have said no?
Hello when goodbye would have been wiser,
I'll do it someday rather than now.
The will is the starter of each project and decision exhibiting
                    personal authority

Do we give ourselves over to spouse, relationship, wine,
sex, drugs, or church?
Yoga, running, eating, nature, or too much work?

Internal choices display
                external authority

Then times of undoing, also a choice
a will-driven decision to not engage,
to sit, not run, to hide for a while.
What prompts these inner dictates, is there
                another authority?

Is there an "inner voice," a spiritual understanding that
Enriches the decisions, choices and tendencies,
a voice that awakens our ability to comprehend
what is truth or true to oneself?
Is there a supreme will guiding decision making,
                a higher authority?

Is there a surrendering at some deep level
to a divine order that helps us run our lives
efficiently, with harmony and timelessness?
Is there a divine plan or path to follow,
                a living authority?

It seems so,
for where my little will bows to a wiser will
and my true identity, more clearly
comes forth,
And I more easily relax into a larger, wiser
unnamed prompting from the unseen,
but deeply felt
                eternal authority

CINDERELLA IMPRINT

I love the idea of a relationship,
envisioning joyous compatibility
laughter, free and easy romance,
meaningful communications
    on every level.

Wonder-filled traveling together
relaxed authentic mutuality,
interchange of ideas and interest,
a kind, generous, fabulous gentleman
    who adores me.

Funny fun kindness that governs
an expansive heart and mind.
Oh, most important, intelligent
with wisdom and compassion
    sprinkled with spirituality.

Yes, a perfect love affair
spontaneously living out loud,
such a glorious idealization ...
then all around past memories
    dampen the dream.

Flooding recollections, past experiences,
conversations and observations,

yes, those happily coupled give question
actually, pause button quickly pushed.
    A fantasy or reality?

Another voice in my head or heart,
"Why, oh why would I want to
disrupt my lovely life
for a dream, a fantasy, childhood story?"
    Hmmm, something to ponder …

CHAPTER 3

THE SACRED PATH

Walker, Traveler, Pilgrim—Walking Creates the Road

ON THE SACRED PATH

On the sacred path, I listen to my soul
Which speaks to me in a wee, small voice.
    In the quietness and stillness
        Of my inner being
           I listen to the wisdom
        That shares divine choice.

In the sacred place of the most-high Presence,
I reverently come to discover me,
        For in the chambers of the Infinite's heart
           Is where shines the light and I can see.

I listen to my soul on the sacred path;
Here is where I separate wheat from chaff.
        The transformation from confusion to clarity
           Bringing increasing transparency.

PILGRIM WALK

May I be gently led
upon a path unknown.
May my foot find solid ground,
sure footing on this
       Pilgrim Walk.

Life is a Pilgrim Walk,
a sojourn into the veiled mystery,
some paths predictable — school, home;
others spiraling almost treacherously,
       the Pilgrim Walk.

Preparing for the journey,
have my choices been sound?
Am I equipped to make this trek?
What's awaiting to be found
       on the Pilgrim Walk.

Once eyes have gazed upon
a far horizon beckoning,
how can adventure be denied.
Inner urging to do what calls
       is Pilgrim Walk.

In order to walk towards,
one must walk away
creating a void, letting go
of familiar, rote, predictability.
       Take Pilgrim Walk.

There are retchings of uncertainty,
spasms of mistrust of one's self.
The void appears empty, lifeless.
But nature's way is to fill space
on Pilgrim's Way.

Intentions, goals are fine
without action are meaningless,
until space is created for something new.
Routine, boredom, sameness is not
the Pilgrim Way.

Freedom calls, time for oneself.
No obligatory appearances.
Integrity with self, calls deep and clear.
Demeaning does not resonate with the
divine Pilgrim Way.

The pull is too great to retrace my steps;
what once was fun has become less.
Where passion flowed now has slowed.
Time to find a newness and beginning.
True Pilgrim Walk.

THE VOICE

As a child, I heard that voice.
A simple "no" is what I recall
but clear impulse in my ear.

I don't remember when it stopped,
seven or eight, I think.
At first, I did not notice
until a long time had passed
      and no voice did enter.

It seemed so natural.
I guess it was part of being human
and that everyone had this presence,
      near and always tender.

That was long ago, and no more,
a voice audible companion.
Perhaps it was just training to know
      my ever-present eternal center.

SONG OF THE ANCIENTS

Middle of the night meditation a few days ago —

Behind me they stand
    like shadowy, not quite clear figures,
a long line of ancestral grandmothers
    sending their accumulated wisdom
        strength and sacred thoughts collectively,
            forward to those of us standing in this
            pivotal time.

Their wisdom, distilled by toil, tears, loving
    from many varying lifetimes'
        experiences, ravages and triumphs.
These ancient ones and more closely related presences
    sending support and encouragement into a world
        desperate for the light gleaned through galaxies
        both near and far.

These souls come now to us at this time
    to champion the arising workers of light
        with song, dance, expanding shifts in
        the cosmology
            long entranced upon the masculine
            structures
                created on Earth.

The foundations are crumbling as the songs
of the sacred feminine
    voices arise to see the walls tumble like Jericho of old.
        Prayer praise power from centuries
        of yin energies stored,
            collecting now being channeled
            through those
                listening receptacles
                of rebalancing energies.

Millions of soul lights igniting around the planet
    shifting at unseen levels,
        strengths that are now appearing in form
        and positioning.
Listen, listen to the ancient ones as they chant us into
a new day!

Many children now entering through women's sacred bowls
    are dedicated karmic-free individual souls coming
        to assist in helping bring forth a new
        creative society,
a world that endeavors to work for all,
    not the greedy few grasping for goods and power,
        a planet where all are honored, empowered
        as holy souls.

A refined beautiful simplicity arises to heal Mother Earth
    restoring balance between both necessary,
    yang and yin,
        we all being male and female needing
        to stand equal

with interior parts being brought
into harmony
through reflected plentitude into
the workings
of the entire world and its
various peoples,
balance, symmetry and finally
peace
for every living thing.

This is the Song of the spheres being sung into our universe
to enter hearts and minds by the long line
of ancestors
standing strongly behind us in varying
shapes and
soul expressions vibrating at a
new intensity,
shattering the old that the new ancient wisdom may
come forth
as the grandmothers of old hear the crying
of the children
and have come to help, to love, mending
the torn fabric
of this world and bring it back
to equality
of mutual caring and sharing.
The way of the ancient wisdom in modern adornment,
regal, poised, gracious and most powerful of all loving
love resulting in equilibrium in the natural world,
a healthy ebb and flow of mutual
cooperative support.

Show us the way
Light our path
Sing your songs
Chant melodies through us out into every corner
of the Earth.

We are ready to tip the scales of imbalance to a planet
    where all can live in safety, satisfying harmony,
        work to care for their own beloveds
            by helping others, we heal our hearts
            and minds.
Gratitude flows to all those who have proceeded us
    knowing we are never alone
        but supported by countless unseen witnesses.

        Sing, grandmother, sing the song
        of our freedom!

THE UNFOLDING

Opportunities are like pregnant pauses
in the hypnotic routine
a field of yet-to-be-discovered treasurers of untold kinds.
Opportunity is an open invitation to step forward into life
        in a new and expanding way.
An opportunity needs recognition, or it slips elsewhere
for another.

The Unknown is the mystery and mythos of living,
to feel the nerve endings alive with a little fear
and excitement.
We are blindfolded to the future and see by taking the next
        indicated hesitant or anxious step.
The Unknown beckons, "Come," singing, "Yes, you can!"

The Unfolding of life is a mystical journey into newness;
rare and choice are these times in our lives when desire calls.
To step forward not knowing the course this pilgrimage
will take
        is a courageous first step into the unknown,
allowing, letting, breathing, patiently the unfolding will occur.

In these times of unknowing, it takes a hardy heart
going forth.
Life shifts come in many different packages—career, love, art.
But if one does not explore the mystery at life's end
        the haunting ... "what if I'd ..." will be more painful
        than trying
for regrets are acutely agonizing exceeding overcoming fear.

Embrace these visitations, trembling perhaps but stepping
onto ground
that has not yet been tested but will in some mysterious way
hold you and guide you unto an unexpected path
      that expands, blesses, enriching the soul journey.
Is winning or losing, still a richer gain?

By touching that spiritual place deep within,
there reverberates throughout one's inner world
that perhaps not too familiar sensation
      expanding, exploding into every direction,
the sacred golden flame's luminosity now radiantly burning.

DANCING FEET

Life evermore spinning in
eternal twists and turns,
a dervish dance of harmony and
discordant notes,
a speeding and receding
forward and back.
      Life is an awkward dance.

My feet falter at the new routine.
Unfamiliar, the rhythm and
pace causes uncertainty.
Willingness driving the parade
again until at last
a comfortable familiarity and
beauty of movement ensues.
      Life is a lovely dance.

So familiar the twirls and turns.
Not much thought is needed.
Then, abruptly new steps
introduced, I stumble,
uneasy at awkward way
of being until once more I learn.
      Life is an ever-shifting dance.

Dance, gypsy, dance.
Embrace each partner anew.
Dip and sway like a limber twig.
Come out from formality
And learn to play.
　　　Life can be a joyous dance.

Eschew the dirge with heavy feet.
Lighten your steps and tap.
Loosen your clothing, bare your feet.
Dance in the rain, sand and soil.
　　　Make life an adventurous dance.

For in the dance, the body knows,
from early childhood, how to sway.
Release your uptight stiffened way.
Become supple, a body, mind
and soul loosen.
　　　Awake to the mystery of a new dance.

RAIN WALKING

Rain walking —
    is a wonderful thing to do.
        The air is so fresh and
            the world gray but new.

I can almost hear the growing
    of roots and plants
        as spring prepares
            to bless with a surprise or two.

JOURNEYS, PILGRIMAGES, PASSAGES OF SEASONS

Relationships woven into the fabric of an individual life lived
with an inquiring spirit and integrity
to best of one's ability at each step on the path.
    The footsteps created a path through the turning
    of seasons,
        the path became the road,
            the road defined much of the life,
                one simple unobserved step at a time.
                There is no other way.

The sights, sensations that arrested my attention
may be very different than others,
the uniqueness of personal pilgrimage experiences.
    Having an unquenchable curiosity
        for the undercurrents of consciousness
            that create the stream, that carry cultures
            forward or backward.

A great fascination even as a small child
    though I could not have then articulated such.
        A child only knows to wonder why.
            Maturing enables the identification
            of patterns, energies
                that appear to be cause to the
                effect evidenced.

Being an observer, even unknowingly
    builds an inventory of impressions, thoughts,
        wonderings that somehow organize themselves
            into plausible possibilities, finally
            conclusions.
                Conclusions always open
                to modification.

A favorite learned life tool has been
the "inquiry basket" taken from
a communications workshop of Werner Erhard's work.
When confronted with a new piece of information,
concept, postulated truth or fact
not to immediately accept as true
because someone saying it's true,
and not to dismiss, reject or scoff
at an unfamiliar idea.

Hmmm, interesting. Let's see ...
Put into the "inquiry basket" for a while.
If relevant to my unfolding learning
more facts revealing it as plausible or phony.
True or false come to my understanding,
then choosing my own conclusion,
accumulating pieces of life's puzzle
gaining wisdom along the long walk.

This is more than an open mind
where everything can enter, and also fall out,
a part of the human long learning process.
Sometimes these things drop out of the basket
seemingly no relevance to my sphere of interest,
not worthy of pursuing in any way,
becoming a deep inner intuitive work
rather than a conscious
studiousness.

Heavens knows, we are constantly surrounded
with seeming facts of all sorts, thus discrimination in
choosing where to spend mental time is a personal
examination.
For this reason, some of us forsook television years ago.
The clutter in the mind and emotional system too acute
being able to sense clearly the lies being
perpetrated by
political bias of so-called news, slants,
propaganda
made me wildly angry, not my
emotional state of choice.

Realizing this was not good for my well-being,
desiring not to have this bad news box at home,
a sanctuary of peace, beauty and silence.
These are footsteps I have taken, and continue to take,
creating aspects of the journey.
The road has defined the life
one unobserved step at a time.
Footsteps are the only way.

WANDERING

I wonder where I wander ...
        where I have wandered
                and will continue to wander.
                        Where is the clearly marked path?
                        Where are the road signs
                                that prompt me to go or stay?

Where are the voyagers
        coming with me on this journey?
                Where is the signpost, I pray?

A wanderer wandering,
        wandering in circle and ovals,
                wandering up the hill, familiar,
                        and into the valleys well known.

Wandering the dusty red road
        as the wise Indians of old would say,
                wandering the clay-baked roads
                        now covered with oil product asphalt.

Wandering,
        wondering,
                having good days and dull,
                        having peaks and valleys,
                                never being fully in the know.

Where, oh where is that guide divine
    with signs so obvious, I cannot miss
        Where is the voice that shatters the silence?
            Where is my love to walk beside?

I am weary of wandering alone,
    home to empty silent house,
        a dinner scratched from white cartons
            to dine in the aloneness that is mine.

I have wandered far enough.
    I have wandered and proven myself.
        Now I long for a companion dear
            to walk with me in this remaining year.

This is the weary cry of my heart,
    this is my prayer new.
        This is all I have to say,
            an inner desire true.

GENERATIONAL CURSE

Is it the way the wind whips across the land
    that irritates the inner human?
Is it the way the cold penetrates
    into the very bone
that causes the human
    to feel alone?

What fury hides within the hearts
    of those who are brothers?
What fury lies within the bosom
    of sisters and others?

From what deep well of
    unheard curses rise into the day
where once there was love
    now seemingly all swept away?

What songs could heal the tribes
    of all humankind?
What dance could loosen the
    fury into a new mind?

What gentle touch could soothe
    the enraged passions?
What thought could begin
    the forgiving of nations?

If I do not begin with me
        how can I expect more of you?
If I cannot forgive and find peace
        how can inner peace come due?

Do we find some satisfaction
        in our anger and turmoil?
Is the feeling so familiar
        making forgetting a toil?

Every day is the scab picked anew,
        the wound ever festering within.
Is this hatred and anger,
        what the prophets, pundits call sin?

Surely, we can find a new and better way
        to show our children how to live this life
with some joy, peace and contribution
        rid at last of anger, hatred and strife.

Walk a new path for your feet to follow,
        forge a new, pleasant terrain.
Find a forest or glen, seashore or stream
        there your thoughts retrain.

Oh, sweet spirit of all,
        you who sing the songs of peace.
Enter our hearts anew,
        giving us that precious release.

Is it the wind that whispers a lie,
  when within sweet water speaks truth?
To what shall we listen, the hate or the love?
  That which we choose gives the proof.

For our choices are made evident
  in the results of our lives.
The window of our soul
  reveals our nature to all eyes.

The wind can lie,
  the elders could be wrong,
but the soul tells the truth.
  Pure essence sings our song.

Tell a new story,
  sing a new song.
Make a new choice
  for generations long.

INNER ROAD TO OUTER PATH

Is it the time to walk away
    from something else in life?
A subtle nudge arising, social convenience,
    old routine or habit, conviviality challenged?
Does it bring forth false personality or persona,
    obscuring the authentic?
Is this a long-sought soul request?

Feeling resistance to being part of
    a whole way of being in community,
yet, a number of creatives have broken the mold,
    no longer being a participant
nor part of daily pattern.
    Many seem to have gone on, uncomfortably,
with their lives, shunning dependences of old routines.

Is this the time that is calling for
    inner and outer integrity?
Transparency? Allowing only the authentic
    to now arise,
not blurred by substance dampening
    the voice that wants to speak
an honest true statement to the world?

That road is not yet visible.
    Others have created their own pathways
By taking steps to a far horizon they desire to reach.
    One shall not know that road —

the Camino de Personal, without walking
        each footfall by themselves.
That path becomes the road leading to
        a not yet discovered destination.

The road is made by walking; there is no other way.
        One cannot fly to that unknown place.
No maps to follow, only one's own internal guidance system
        heeding the inner promptings,
listening to voice with no volume
        being present into this day, this footstep,
this next indicated life step.
        There is no road, traveler.

Being mindful of the inner prompts
        and outer signposts,
one finds their way, one step at a time,
        one day, one moment, a breath, inhale, exhale,
until looking over your shoulder, seeing the path
        where one's footsteps shall never fall again.
What lies behind in past. What lies ahead, revealed by
        embracing the seductive mystery.
A destiny created by walking ...
        seems there is no other way.

Things too heavy or cumbersome for the journey
        are discarded along the way.
First the lesser unimportant baggage in a moment,
        eventually, the hidden things surface, beginning
        to irritate,

reluctantly are deemed too detrimental to carry any longer
affecting health or well-being.
Walker chooses the higher road allowing these long-
embedded habits,
ways of maneuvering to fall away lightening
the journeying.

Freed from the cumbersome rituals, habitual denials,
a new wind blows, the road opens into territories
of possibilities
not yet seen or offered before.

The road is made by walking, listening, responding,
taking the path called forth.
The next indicated step, thus so it goes.
There is no other way.
Traveler, there is no road.
Your road is created by walking
your own way.

CHAPTER 4

SOLE TO SOUL

One Unrepeatable Step at a Time

SOUL JOURNEY

Soul journey is walking a path unknown.
The path must step around rocks,
      climb over or through obstructions,
         like a river of peace
            flowing around boulders
               over hard places—
                  no resistance.

The road is made by the path
    we chose to step upon,
        not fighting obstacles,
           finding the way of peace
             within oneself
               as much as possible.

The journey begins with a step.
    Steps create a path.
        Walking makes the road.
           There is no other way.

COME AWAY, MY LOVELY

come away, my lovely,
come sit barefoot upon my breast
feel the pulse of my presence
let the cool earth awaken your long exploring feet

come away, my lovely,
sit upon the softness of my sands
run your fingers through millions of particles of my
        unique surface
let the waters of my ocean body bathe you in a baptism
        of pure aliveness
cleansing, washing away the dust of worry or regret
        that accumulated in rote dailiness

come away, my beloved,
walk my mountain paths, savor the air, scent of the forest,
        revel in old growth trees
stretch your limbs, embrace my beauty
climb upon a large rock feeling its ancient strength
        holding you, warming you in my sunlight
marvel at the eons of time all has been here
allowing the silence to seep into your pores

come away, my lovely,
be amazed by the ethereal stretch of sands upon my
        great tan and purple deserts
marvel at the hardiness of resilient plants and
        various creatures, hidden and visible

sit upon my warm body, sift sand and draw a great circle
        around yourself, and know you are also the center

come to realize, my lovely,
that this very moment is my epicenter, my source of
        planetary forces, one of many great vortexes
allowing these geometrically designed forces
        to be a part of you, as they are
open to the energies, gentle yet forceful beyond
        comprehension,
being in constant motion, like your own body cells,
also, my oceans, clouds, subterranean forces, winds, rains,
        storms, weather patterns of every description
feel this dynamic, be it, for so you are

drink in the verdant life force of a primordial forest
the cycle of life so evident
from acorn to sapling to great monumental
        king of the grove
eventually dying process, falling, decaying
creating fungal soil for newer oaks to grow
you, too, are this

touch my frozen surface
marvel at the range of temperatures on the planet
ponder the icy watery home to adaptable hardy life
the slow melting of this white land flooding lakes,
        streams rivers and shorelines
filling aquifers, reservoirs beneath earth's surface
my lovely, you are also this, being filled by my bounty

marvel at the foods, resources growing across my surface
many varying soils and climates, night, day, seasons
producing everything you need to eat, drink, wear, live in
every substance of natural origin originates from my body

i am your mother
the ethers, heavens are your father
our union is your universal stars, moon, galaxies
        all one living organism
created from a template of pure loving expression
an ongoing expansion of evolutionary process
never ceasing, only changing with each moment
you are all of this

my lovely, become aware of your true magnificent self
awaken to your own cosmology,
be aware of my patterns of energy.
repose daily upon my body of sand, grass, soil, or rock
        feel my heartbeat of passion
singing a melody of pure eternal unity
come to me often, my lovely, come.

EMBRACING THE MYSTERY

What calls or is there a call?
What wants to show itself?
What is the distancing within
toward everything that was?

Starting a journey on unmarked path
is a walk of faith into the unknown.
Perhaps there is truth in knowing
all is unknown.
Only mystery is cause.

We think we know, but do we?
We think we have it all in life
then comes an abrupt change,
nothing remains just as it was.

There is uncertainty in every day
perceived or not, beneath all lies
similarity and predictability, we like
surprises, tragedy, upset our laws.

We thought we had control,
how wrong, mistaken we are.
Control is an illusion of self
within mystery, contemplatively we pause.

So, the journey is an acknowledgement
that the mystery is being embraced,
willing to feel uncertain shifts, once stuck
into newness on ashes of what was.

THE LABYRINTH

The Labyrinth — a metaphor for life,
for the Journey,
    straight forward the entry
    soon to take a turn left.
        A sense of this is the way
        then a turning again
            a returning.

Am I going backwards?
A sharp angle and the direction shifts
    and so does my path.
    An opening, a flow.
        "Oh, this is my way."

Then a sharp turn
an unexpected reversal.
    The direction seems incorrect
    yet the path beckons on.

Again, a corner to be turned,
a short sojourn to another direction.
    I am confused.
    Will I ever find my way?
        Again, around and an opening
        striding confidence returns.

There is an ease, a looking up to gaze about
then the journey abruptly takes me in a new direction.
> The changes come more quickly, sharply.
> I feel almost lost.
> > And then, I enter the center,
> > feeling an ecstasy
> > > a triumphant exhilaration
> > > a resting.

But it is not a place to long remain.
Again, the pathway calls.
> My reluctant foot stretches forward
> to begin again.

The Path takes me from center
to the outer edges of undefined mystery
> then called in once more
> to twists and turns,
> > almost back to center,
> > then out again.

Each step has built trust in the process
of being a sojourner
> on the path,
> undefined, yet
> > carefully laid before
> > the seeking.

In the passage of time the return becomes clear
and the end is in sight.
　　With reluctance
　　glancing back
　　　　at the circuitous pilgrimage.
Gratitude and remorse!
Expectance and trust.
　　The Path leads to where it began
　　and there is no place to go
　　　　but to return home.

Leaving this evolutionary journey,
　　accepting the plan
　　　　surely came though diversity.

Perceiving variety behind difference,
needful purpose of unknowing
　　in aspects of the outer
　　to sense the matrix
　　　　governing inwardly
　　　　　　the unfolding path.

IN THE KINGDOM OF DIVINE LOVE,
THERE IS NO CHASTISEMENT

There is no chastisement within divine love.
>There is no damning or criticism, no rebuke,
>or admonishments.
Only seeing what is possible within each soul,
>visioning the original template brought into being
>at the Dawn of Creation.

A beautiful human journey to unfold like a flower
through present
>life experiences on Earth and toward the waiting
>kingdom of eternity,
where great lessons from your template are revealed
>and brought forth in your Earth walk.

On one side of the veil of eternal existence, one can gaze upon
>that template of one's individual vision
imbedded into the heart-mind, brought into being
>by the creator for each soul ever created.

One can realize how in the last incarnation one may have
missed the mark
>but never a sin, just a child learning to maneuver onto
>a higher path
on the long road to the kingdom of eternity.
>All journeys are made one step at a time.

Endeavoring in this, gazing upon the blueprint of oneself,
>how to walk a higher road of learning

releasing, conforming to the faint memory
        of the original template of who one truly is meant to be.

The Earth fosters human forgetting, yet there are nudges
of intuition,
        mirrors in others—family, teachers, words that
        awaken something deep within,
suffering illness, joys and sorrows, soul friends returning
into one's personal orbit,
        almost immediately stimulating another part
        of ourselves.

We do not always understand this is divine guidance,
        knowing our desire to choose a higher more
        productive good.
Thus, the meditative page of sacred time each day is just
such a choice well made,
        as one more clearly recognizes one's truer self, leaving
        one more enriched,
guided, kindly enlightened counseled by that infinite
truth within,
        the wisdom ever known yet not yet recognized.

A spiritual practice of expansive order
        is each one's own meditative tool touching once again,
a forgotten wise template of truth for this soul's
        individualized pilgrimage through eternity.

You are always awaited and welcomed with love,
        ever chastisement.
The great presence ever as near as your next breath,
        we are blessed to kindly bless others.

GLORY

On the waves of thought, there are patterns for you to discern.
They are universal patterns. Become aware. You will see them more
and more.

The pattern of light through crystal
    wherein are basic colors — red, blue, yellow, green, violet.
    The movement of the air current animates
    the hanging crystal
    and reflects the glorious colors,
    the swirling spectrum of all color.

The soul is like a crystal.
    When animated by the spirit
    light is allowed to shine into its pure essence,
    the refractory glory is revealed in the person.
    A glow, a beauty that shines from within
    dancing gently into the world.

Moments of magic,
    miracles unfolding.
    In ordinary circumstances
    glory revealed.

"Go to the light!
Come daily and bask.
The unseen elegantly animates all."

A WALK CELEBRATING AGELESSNESS

It was that time of leaving and arriving together,
    not taking the Camino at this pivotal time in my life.
    But instead, a walk, a solitary yet crowded roadway,
        a half marathon in the freezing cold dark morning
        in the Nevada desert.

Dropped off...awaiting the gunshot
    that would set adrenaline rushing.
    The first step, those faithful feet stretching forth,
        takes the muscles cold, constricted as
        the journey begins.

Footfall after footfall, the stride begins to lengthen,
    the inner heat starting to build
    a release of tight shoulders pulled up toward ears
        hands unclenching and legs stretching like
        a lovely thoroughbred filly
        warming to the race.

Then cotton gloves, warming slightly the frosty morning
    Temperature tossed to the side of the road.
    In time, the outer layer of warmth is added
        by the walking.
            Running parade of many
            deep breathing bodies.

The darkness is being pierced by the first darts of light
　　　like rips shredding a dark cloth
　　　more strides, more footfalls
　　　　　a sense of inner rhythm playing
　　　　　　　its own music.

Others come alongside to chat or briefly
　　　connect, then onward.
　　　As one's own interior energy
　　　　　builds and presses on leaving those
　　　　　　　passing faces behind.

Now the vest is tossed like a rich princess flinging her ermine
　　　onward, light illuminating the glow of morning
　　　more exertion to overcome the slight slant of the road
　　　　　cresting the rim and below awakening
　　　　　with lights flickering bathed in rose gold.
　　　Las Vegas like a lovely ruin appearing,
　　　　　a great city that once was.

Slowly increased brilliance from the rising sun
　　　dispels any mystical vision of another time and place.
　　　Yet from miles away, watching this city
　　　　　of glitz and glamour, sham and sin,
　　　　　looking somewhat innocent
　　　　　　　as a sleeping child just awakening.

The sun begins to make her radiance felt.
    The last possible garment of excess clothing
    is tossed upon the material littered roadside.
        I hear that thrift and charity shops reap
        the harvest of discarded clothing,
        somehow adding another delight to this,
          my birthday, February 3,
          celebrating agelessness
          for Grand Patty, a great grandmother.

In time, I hear the music and cheers of the awaiting
    celebratory receiving committee.
    I think of the chip they placed on the shoelace
    of my marathon shoes
        in case it was necessary to know
        who is this fallen one.

But not today, oh grateful joy!

RELEASING AND ALLOWING

Releasing and allowing a life of deep surrender.
Letting the past pass,
opening gently to what appears
        allowing what is mine to come to me.

No clear roadmap, only openings small.
A choice of paths and forks,
feeling my way like a blind child,
        amazed at what comes to me.

An invitation here, a nudge there,
a reacquaintance with a new idea.
Space and quiet nothingness.
Unfamiliar rhymeless dance,
        what will come to me?

Open and receptive to discovery
willing to release what does not serve.
Choice of exclusion and inclusion,
sorting, shaking, evaluating, awaiting
        who or what wants to come to me?

Portals open and in floods light,
portals close banning familiar sight.
Unseen forces swirling about,
energies shifting quietly – no shout
        revealing what is to come to me.

Is this not how life unfolds?
No great, clear vision of forever?
Glimpses, intuitions, synchronicities
bringing in the unexpected occurrences,
        allowing them to come to me.

When I decide how it should look
or reason how it is to be,
too rigid, the blinders to glimpse
what wants to present itself
        and come easily to me.

THE WALK OF A THOUSAND VEILS

This morning, this day in a new and powerful way
   gently, the forces of Unseen Presence
walk with me to new territories,
    vistas appearing to my, before now, blind sight.

It is all there and has always been.
   I now approach with awe and wonder.
How could I have not seen what is now so clear?
    This moment is my new year.

My soul responds with quiet joy
   vibrating to the newness of this day.
Treasures long sought appear by the way
    always available until, I in realization say,
"All is mine that I have ever desired."

The treasures we seek are the treasures that seek us.
   The wonders of life have always been,
yet in a twinkling of an eye, the fog seems to lift
    and crystal clear what I sought does appear.

Yet now I see through a veil darkly.
   But one day, today, tomorrow and each day to come,
I shall see as I am seen
    for all I see is still a reflection of me.

So, may I clean my glass a little more this day.
   May the clarity of inner sight grow stronger.
May I drop my self-imposed blinders and see anew,
    for in all, I seem to find You.

FINGERS IN THE DIRT

I have always a strong longing to place
    my fingers in the dirt.
It is my leveling place between the frantic pace
    and finding that sweet, inner face.

I have often the desire to place my fingers
    deep into the soil.
It is my therapy, my art form, my physical
    excursion that is joy, not toil.

My hands love the dirt, the clay and the
    grainy, sun-bleached beach sand.
This is a place where Earth reaches
    Heaven right in my very own hand.

The fruit of my labors shows so brilliantly
    in the colors dancing upon green stock.
My flowers and foliage are my reward
    wearing their best brilliantly attired frock.

My fingers love to dive in clay
    wet and slippery, I revel to play,
to fashion a bowl, a cup or plate
    my hands in outward form to pray.

My need to touch the earth
    almost every newborn morn
cutting a rose, removing a thorn
    weeding, digging, my soul adorn.

To commune with nature
    fingers in the dirt,
for me is like touching
    the Divine's skirt.

Laid like mantle over hills
    and shore
I must touch you, Creator
    And listen to your song.

SUNDAY MORNING SILENCE

Planting a seed is a holy act.
Placing a nondescript seed into the ground
is an act of faith —
    faith that it will germinate
    faith that it will grow
    faith that one day your garden will receive blooms
        perfumed from where?
        colored by whom?
        vitality from what source?

Planting a garden with various small dark dots of potentiality
acknowledging the life force resident in all of nature's
many wonders,
we dig the dirt, place the promise into the dark,
water and wait.
How like life this is.
    We think a thought
    perhaps pray, intend, or hope
    having taken the action, we now release, waiting ...
        and one day the thing strangely manifests.
        Who arranges these things?
        Where do unfulfilled hopes and dreams go?
        From where do new aspirations arise?

Ah, sweet mystery of life, has been spoken many times
in many different ways and tongues,
yet it is the thing of good stories, sometimes called miracles.

But are they miracles, or
        just the law of life working?
        Life creating itself out of itself?
        Expansion, the cosmos is always occurring.
                Shift happens, and then happens again, they say.
                What is the force behind all movement —
                The stars, moon, oceans, air, comets,
                babies growing in the womb?

Eternal inquiries floating in the collective consciousness
needing to be answered,
not by others, just ourselves.

I DANCE ON THE EDGE OF YOUR DREAMS

In the dark night hours
I tiptoe onto the edge of your dreams
hoping to arrest your attention,
longing for love's soul schemes.

On the edge of deepest sleep,
my soul escapes and travels
far and wide; there is a mystical search.
The intricacy of separation unravels.

In the wee hours just before dawn,
can you not catch a glimpse of me?
Awaken, beloved; send your soul to meet mine.
May our journeys now intertwine.

In the deepest of sleep,
I dive and soar through eternity.
Ages are all a continuum of play.
I frolic from a past to a present identity.

Come, beloved, join my dance.
Come hear the music my soul sings.
Come back, come forth.
Come rise up from your bed.
My spirit calls to your spirit.
Come dear one, and we shall wed.

Wed as the stars wed in the sky
the sand is caressed by the sea
as the giant oak roots invade the earth,
so your being in ecstasy permeates me.

Find me today where I hide.
Map a destiny our love to bring.
You are my dream held long inside.
Then in unison, our hearts to sing.

Find me today where I am.
You are the dream I have dreamed
throughout the ages.
Come, dearest, this very day.
Fill at last our empty pages.

I come, I am dancing
here on the edge of your sleep.
Arise, beloved, rise, come,
in joyous union keep.

In a primordial ecstasy, we shriek,
yes, to our union, blissful repass.
Yes, yes to life and love,
awaken, awake, at last.

CHAPTER 5

PORTALS AND PASSAGES

Foam Trails Upon the Sea, Then Gone

PORTAL

My head slowly turns toward the awaiting portal
Where the light calls me, and I am ready.
Open door to a larger expression of the mystery,
      Finally willing to enter into the luminous Unknown.

Naked I stand. Of course, naked, bare, empty-handed
Heart-mind, head-mind cleansed, empty of yesterdays.
Holding nothing, taking nothing but my purified soul
      Into the luminous light of the unknown.

BIRTHING PORTAL

A portal — the birth channel
     of the psyche
The natural maturational
     path to rebirth
Transformational platform comes
     from passion
     into maturation
     incubation
     isolation
     reflection
     metamorphism

Until the urgency of new life
     pushes itself through
     the passageway
     from unseen
     to seen

From unmanifest
     to manifest
     and the transformational
     moment arrives

The butterfly emerges
     the new thing is seen
     a fresh vital life,
     idea, relationship
     has been formed

And birthed through
        the portal
        of what was,
        becomes the dream
        of unlimited potentiality.

Jesus spent much of his time communing with his own soul; for it is through our inner thoughts that we contact the Infinite. To this remarkable man, out of the silence of his own soul, came a direct revelation of his sonship, his Oneness with what he called the Father.

Back of all conflict of ideas, back of the din of external life and action, life is resisting and succumbing to portals of many kinds.

MYSTICAL PORTALS

The changes and shifts
      along life's path unavoidable,
      arrive through
            mystical portals.

From baby to child
      child to teen, then to young adult,
      to maturity, each journey through
            mystical portals.

These openings unseen
      deeply felt are the pilgrimages
      orchestrated by the soul
            progressive portals.

Times when constriction almost crushes,
      times when expansion exhilarates,
      each maturation on a path trod through
            mystical portals.

Opening the inner wisdom being called forth
      moving into experience
      unlike any other, by way of
            infinite portal.

Naked I stand before the celestial portal.
      Naked each will stand one day,
      the last day, this portal
            will return no more.

For each must travel
        to the unknown place
        through the final
                mysterious portal.

The open anticipatory entry,
        each encounter is a pregnancy of the unknown,
        a moment of urgency to push forward into
        the confronting
                mystical portal.

all must encounter,
        for each life has its own
        soul journey through
                eternity's portal.

Ode to Painting —

"MONASTERY OF OLDE"

How I long to reach that shore
Rough sea journey in a small boat
Touching ground of my own being
     Finding monastery of olde.

Tiny vessel touching unfamiliar land
Joyously leaving watery waves behind
Foot resting, illumination by golden hue
     Lighting monastery of olde.

Pyramid of luminosity
Embraces isle remote
With radiant powerful glow
     Awakening monastery of olde.

Swirling forces seen and unseen
Ever unfolding expanding energy
Over which there is no control
     By small monastery of olde.

Weather occurring, ages long
Awaiting visitors who dare
Explore rough seas and land
     Find their monastery of olde.

Here is where the secrets reside
Memories of all that have been
Sheltered by the radiant light
     My soul monastery of olde.

NAKED I STAND

Naked I stand
        stripped of old pretense
Unclothed, one realization at a time,
        motives laying bare my soul.

Naked I stand
        before the sun, scorched
By the searing light,
        truth laying bare my soul.

Naked I stand
        unadorned of old illusions
Of grandeur's deceit,
        reality laying bare my soul.

Naked I stand,
        unclothed by time's passage
Ageless and aging,
        acceptance lays bare my soul.

Naked I stand
        before the world and the Divine,
Liberated from shoulds and woulds;
        freedom now bears my soul.

DARE TO STAND NAKED

Shed your self
Strip away your persona.
Dare to stand naked
    Before heaven and yourself.

Rip away the badges of merit
Cut open the insular suit.
Dare to stand naked
    Before your own amazed eyes.

Silence the stale stories
Mute the old sad songs.
Dare to stand naked
    In the silence whispers a new voice.

A voice silenced for many years
Ancient wisdom longing to be deeply heard.
Naked, dare to listen
    Engaging your slumbering mind.

Stop, cease, let go
Of the tyranny of the urgent.
Dare to not do the frantic pace
    That feels like life, counterfeit life.

Toss away the watch, surrender.
Dissolve the unknown abysses,
Naked, vulnerable self
    That longs to finally come forth.

Shed yourself, public and secret.
Discard your accolades and riches.
Be willing to be nothing, so something
		Fresh, newly naked can emerge.

Naked, stripped, ripped, unadorned.
Silenced, quieted, no point to drive home.
Dare, dare to meet this true self
		That has waited for you so long.

Naked, unscheduled, impressionable,
Bare, free before heaven
And oneself,
		Clothed in peaceful purity.

A long time coming to be able to welcome the new.
Many sad days and painful nights of uncertainty.
Clouded vision, unclear dreams, stuck and afraid
		Now anticipatory excitement embraces
		Unknowingness.

BEYOND MYSTICAL PORTAL

Naked I stand
        tentatively resigned
on my earthly journey,
before looms
        a mystical portal.

Naked I wait again
        unsure of my next
indicated life step,
only my head turned
        facing mystical portal.

How many times
        have I had to quiver,
afraid to move forward
knowing I could not go back
        before mystical portal?

Yet each was a newness
        a journey fresh
more vital than before;
courage arising, to enter
        awaiting mystical portal.

Is this the journey of life,
        the soul having its expression?
Go here, not there. Yes, no.
Guidance unheard but deeply sensed
        leading to mystical portal.

This time seems different,
        no driving adventure beckoning.
Is it resignation or uncertainty
holding me back from
        entering the mystical portal?

Yet standing on rugged rocks,
        feet bloody from resistance
causes remembrance of other crossings.
Gratitude recalled for stepping
        into mystical portal.

Only the promise of a new love
        draws me onward.
I could crumble and fall;
a luminous light beckons
        from mystical portal.

Where will it lead?
        What will be my fate?
Stripped of yesterday's garb
what adornment awaits
        beyond mystical portal?

A NAKED RAW PRAYER

Naked my heart
Naked my mind
Naked my life,
  Raw before my soul.

You have the infinite eyes
  to see deep within.
You have the everlasting wisdom
  that looks at my heart.
You are the creator
  and the sustainer.

Naked I stand ever
  before eternity
Hiding nothing,
  concealing no hidden things,
Open like an apple, sliced
  revealing seed, shape, and fruit.

It is a wonderous thing
  to be known completely,
And loved,
  warts and wonders
Faults and fair qualities.

Before thee
  naked I stand.
It is a goodly thing.
  Great gratitude emerges —

TURN SIDEWAYS INTO THE LIGHT

When those arrive on the field of life
ready to demean, hurt or harm
array thyself in beautiful attire, regal
refusing to have that conversation,
turn sideways into the light
and disappear

Refuse to grovel or sulk,
scrambling for position like seagulls
scurrying on the beach, wrestling
for a scrap of nourishment,
turn sideways into the light
and soar

There are other fields of engagements,
other beaches of plenty
There are worlds within worlds
where attired with grace and beauty
turning toward a beckoning light
you may appear

Just like Jonathan Livingston Seagull
refusing to follow the flock, solo, soaring
into the sky that called strengthening
his solitary flight, relevance was his
appearing at all being called into a
new light

He soared!

PASSAGES INTO A NEW PHASE OF LIFE

Again, over many years I have been laboring there
Now this chapter also is closing
In this particular expression
I lost a spiritual community once before and it caused
Me to grow in unexpected ways
So why not now

I am one with the universe and the universe is one with me
The universe is bursting with new opportunities
Means of involvement
Expression, friends and relevant participation
It is damaging to be where there is no appreciation
for that which
One has to offer
If not appreciated, then one must find a place of pure
expression and
Mutual enlivenment

The deadening repetitive boxes of life that we choose to sit
in are not
To be forever
So I, like Jonathan Livingston Seagull, must learn to use my
solo wings
And see where the currents of wind blow me

When my courage is strong enough to sit in the boat
and then push
Away from the shore I can appreciate some stormy seas
trusting a safe passage
To the land awaiting me

My prophetic painting to which I was so drawn calling me
to make it my own
And bringing it so carefully from Ireland
I have gazed upon it in wondering for
Almost a year and now it begins to reveal itself

No journey is without turbulence; no new horizon is
without some uncertainty
Of its dimensionality, yet I am certain I shall be guided
to what my
Heart calls for at this time in my personal journey
I am not here for hurt and humiliation any longer
I have placed myself in situations that have benefitted me
for a season
But now is time to let go, release and allow, release and allow
A time of surrender and letting go of much I have clung
to that no longer serves
Situations and things need to be allowed to pass
on to others

Bless these years of learning and opportunities that have
now brought
Me to a time I have freedom to choose anew
A time to think, write, teach as opportunity presents itself
Pray as always, all of my life has been dedicated to prayer
for myself, family
And others
Perhaps even that will become richer

I feel more space within me this morning more clarity
and I will wait for the week
My wise friend said to wait before doing anything overt

Thank you, Inner Guidance, for this morning and new courage.

PASSAGE

This is my first consciously accepting day of moving
from one phase of life to another, unknown, mysterious,
and frightening.

Voyages from and voyages to —
the unknown sea churns within a safe harbor
so familiar and well known,
       yet stifling in its predictability
       and waning relevance.

My foot has already stepped into the craft
that will carry me away, and prayerfully,
to some unknown shore
       whose siren song calls me
       to what I do not know.

The rude hurt words upon shore still sting
making the entrance into my unnamed craft easier.
I must flee this season of stifling conformity
       and find my place where
       a peaceful heart can rest.

Years of reading and study
fill mental file drawers
with impressions and remembrances,
concepts, and precepts.
       Praying this day for guidance
       and not foolish emotional reaction.

Some touch deep within ...
and brings Jonathan Livingston Seagull to mind
recalling, "I refuse to be part of the flock
    fighting for food upon the beach.
    I was created to soar."

I refuse to fight for some small territory in an even smaller arena.
I feel the call to soar, and soaring is a solo flight,
be it an outward display of gifts and talents
or a now contemplative life.
    Both are a stretching of inner wings
        to find new skies.
The world is full of new horizons beckoning me strongly.
What is this inner pull
that will not be denied any longer.
    For quite some passage of days, months, years ...
    this nudge has been felt and can no longer be ignored

This push from the shore
has been so unexpected.
    Yet newness calls my soul.
    To a doorway of becoming ...

WHAT NEW DOORWAY BECKONS

What new door beckons, one long ignored?
  If not there but persistently present,
a boundless imagination trumps reality.
  How can trust return, willingness to look?

Take first timid step of inquiry until tried, how to know
what lies beyond the threshold?
  Desire drives the timid soul.

Ask "how?" not "why me?"
  Personal choice steers the ship,
choppy waters, rough and calm
  are the journey that calls forward.

Self-responsibility is one's own hands
  avoiding the rocks of collective opinion,
following the star that calls,
  trusting again the persistent presence.

Not allowing losses takes one down
  "what next?" when looking at the door.
The one most afraid to open
  Is perhaps the very one of desire.

Choice is self-empowerment,
  one avenue blocked find another.
A door slams but there are others.
  Principle in action will win.

STEPS TO UNDERSTAND LIFE PATH

Steps to solutions
Steps to understand life path
Steps, there is no other way
Steps are the building blocks of a life
    one step, one breath, one day creates footprints
        in the sands of soul walk while upon the Earth

No escalators, trains, planes or any vehicle except
the human foot
From first step to last there is only one mental engineer
that runs the
    movement of each thought, word, deed, action
    and footprint
        there is no other

Each is the chooser and the chosen
No matter the intellect, extraordinary or diminished
Choice is still with the mental chooser
Consciously, deliberately, or unconsciously careless
or uncaring
    all still make their own imprint upon
        the path which becomes the road

Yet, paths can be changed or corrected

New territories explored, resulting in a higher road then

previously begun

All lives have opportunities to choose and re-choose

Often as simple as a "yes" or "no"

> both words are a complete sentence

> > steering the compass of living

Each is presented with a fork in the road

The decisions create destination which creates destiny

One step faithfully taken repeatedly becomes the road

There is no other way but a foot stretching forth in

chosen direction

> one breath, one choice, one willing, inquiring,

> > faithful step at a time becomes soul's life path

MY MIND FLUTTERS — THE DREAM

What is my next indicated life step?
Where do I place my foot?
What direction is spirit guiding?
What path should be forsook?

What idea is dancing on the edge of consciousness?
What plan is gestating, waiting to be born?
What word is the key that opens the lock?
What old attitudes to be shredded and torn?

What newness lurks beneath the surface?
Waiting for the old to now pass?
What steps to be taken?
Divine plan in action, at last.

I am expectant of what, I do not know
But the sands of my being are shifting.
In silent mystery in unseen wind,
What was a dune, is now a mountain lifting.

It is as if a tide within recedes without my will.
Slowly, the water's edge creeps away
And then softly comes back again,
Carrying cargo for a new dawning day.

I am pregnant with an unknown dream,
Unknown to my waking mind.
But deep within in silent sleep
The dream I dream, dreams its kind.

That which works within
Will eventually work without.
What lurks in silent secret
Will come forth with a shout.

I am here, do me! I am the very next step.
Of course, you are able, this is what is right,
All the time, energy, ideas and love
Will bring the dream into sight.

I trust in divine process to do the dream.
I trust the unseen to guide me this day.
I trust spirit to scheme the scheme.
I trust Inner Self to birth the dream.

The dream that dreams me
Dreams me to eternity.
That which I know not
Knows that which is sought.

And that which I seek
Seeks me, now complete.
The dream I dream, dreams me!

IRELAND

She found her foot on foreign soils
    secretly imparting her essence,
    a mutual recognition celebrating
    the giving and receiving
    of that sacred land.

The green hills of Ireland
    welcomed her like a daughter
    from days long ago
    a mutual recognition,
    that sacred land.

None walks without leaving a print
    upon the people and lands.
    Encounters etched upon cosmic slate
    those ancient records
    of all sacred land.

She walked sharing what she loved
    and held dear the beauty, mythos, magic
    ancient stories written in stones, hills, wells
    myths still alive in morning dew
    vibrating in sacred land.

She laughed, sang, danced and wept tears
      long harbored in the hidden sea within
      receiving her salty gifts
      kissing her soul with release,
      a gift from sacred land.

She ate bread brown, ale pale
      green of every shade
      sacrificial offerings of hen, lamb, and cattle
      rejoicing, she for beauteous bounty
      of fruitful land.

Swept by winds, rain, hail, and sun
      reshaped her interior regions
      breaking loose long held hurts.
      Vacancies quickly filled with gentle healing
      treading this sacred soil.

TRAVEL

What is it about a vacation?
      Is it not involved in day-to-day-affairs,
      or news, business, world conditions?

No have to's, should's, would's ...
      rather just could.

Could I have a mango or a passion fruit margarita?
      Time for fun, sun, relaxation
      and lots of play.

New tastes, aromas, faces, language
      and, ah, foods
      Fun clothes

Don't just dress
      but costume

I love traveling
      I feel like the family dog
      do you want to ...

I am first one in front seat
      wagging my tail
      let's go

Yes! Yes! Yes!

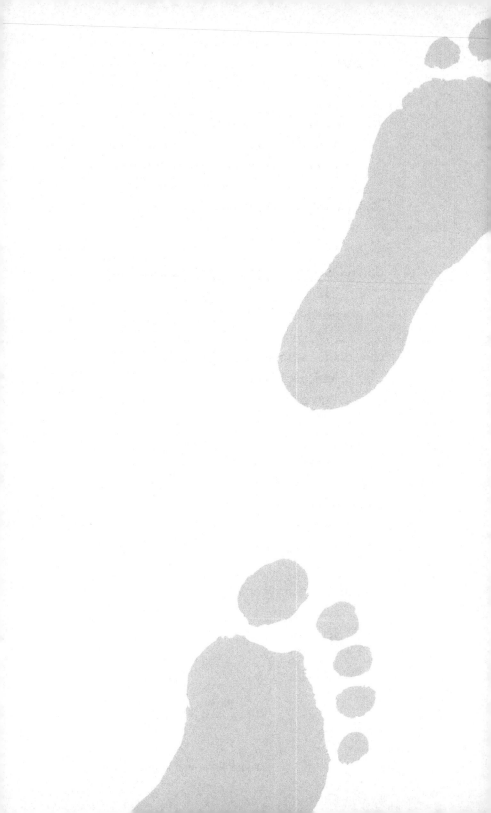

CHAPTER 6

REFLECTIONS OF JOURNEY

The Path Has Made the Road —
There Is No Other Way

I AM THOUSANDS OF WOMEN

I am a thousand women rolled into one.
My roots are long and wide
      touching many countries, cultures and costumes.

The image of grandmothers behind me
trail from the gifts of ten grandchildren
      and soon to be twenty-one great grands.

Back into the very dawn of creation
thousands of brave ancestral women singing their songs
      dancing to their drums, reeds and flutes,

Nursing their babies, touching with healing hands —
capable cooks, weavers, sowers of seeds,
      and oh, the strong bounty of gardeners.

Raising vegetables, fruits, nuts, flowers and grains,
delightful offerings for family, friends and the unseen.
      Spiritual images carried within each precious soul.

Yes, a woman is a composite of thousands of women,
mingling bloodlines, colors and hues, traditions, yet still one,
      there being no racial separation—it is not you or me.
      We are them.

Hurt, hunted, raped and abused, a collective wound we carry,
now a fierce female survivor warrior, lover, mother, sister,
      friend. I am you and you are me.

Together, the divine feminine recognizes herself
seeing that strong line of faithful women in each other.
  We are one and we will reclaim the Earth once more.

In love and well-being for everyone, male and female,
all these generations behind now standing with us
  saying, "Yes, yes you can!" And thus it shall be!

*Note: The Human Genome Project has proven we all carry
the same DNA. There are no separate races, only humanity.
Mongrels, all!*

LIGHT

Everything that exists
appears from darkness.
All seen comes from the unseen.
Out of the seeming void comes the stirring of life.
The universe was dark and without form,
thus, no time which is only the measurement of movement
in space.
      "Let there be light" and the sun came forth.
      "Let there be light" and the Son was created —
One in physical form, the other in the infinite presence.
Both brought light, and life began.

May that same spiritual sun shine this day, bringing perfect
well-being to all systems —
body, mind, spirit, and vision.
      Light shows the way.
      Light warms the day.
      Light illuminates interior darkness
      chasing shadows and gloom away.

      Light births life
      encourages growth,
      lifts the eye and mind,
      promises fruit and flower.

      Light pulses into nature
      mountaintops glistening,
      rainbows and raindrops,
      sunset's glory, sunrise surprise.

      Light is my preference.
      Night has its own kind of beauty
      highlighted by moon glow.
      Shining planets, beckoning stars.

REFLECTIONS
REGARDING STANDING STONE – AGING

Photos do evoke a prompting
the continuation of a name, an ethnic heritage –
Irish, for us so unimportant to the young
more meaningful with maturity
reflective time perhaps looking for assurance of
the continuation of life and all the efforting,
creating a mere ninety or hundred years.

What monuments will stand the testimony
of time spent on this planet?
What enduring evidence that once I roamed
these green hills, black pavement, gray sidewalks
and sandy beaches many?

Footprints quickly fade, words, a few may
endure for a while; memories carried in hearts
of family, loved ones, too
shall pass.

Wooden structures change and eventually
disappear. Stone markers on graves
deteriorate, elements beating upon wear
away words with the passage of time,
then tip and fall, weathered by rain, snow, sun
and even Earth's shifts.

How wise the ancients to place upright
stones of enduring material heralding
their existence even if we only guess
at their meaning or message.
What other purpose did they serve?

A tool of survival, ownership posts,
omens, pillars of power or pride?
Signals of transmitting still and calling
seekers to them in many remote lands?

Perhaps a place of energizing seeds
their means of survival.
Varying shapes and formations, such creative
intensely intricate designs.
How many still hidden, awaiting
curious eye and a reverent touch?

ANCIENT BUBBLES
FROM THE POND OF REMEMBRANCE

In the great pool of stillness
   that long awaiting bubbles of revelatory
understanding,
      are released then slowly, majestically
         rise to the surface.

In the silence of non-doing,
   the practice of gently listening,
      not meditating, contemplating, or thinking.
         Just basking in the soft velvet cloak
            of utter quiet
               then the ancient whisperer
               comes forth.

These are the treasures
   that enrich the storehouse of one's soul.
      The great ones are patient
         waiting perhaps decades for you
            to enter into
               the sanctuary of pure essence.

This is what is wanting to be known.
   Come, dear, to the inner sanctum of silence.
      Breathe, release, allow the calm stillness
         to embrace you.
            You shall know the love
               that passes human understanding.

Come, come away into the quietude that awaits you,
   my beloved, and receive the gifts
   long awaiting your receiving.
      The great secret can only be heard
         deep in the silence of your own soul.

THE GREAT POND OF LIFE

It is a goodly thing to be faithful to the page, going with
a lighter heart
      knowing you are loved and supported.
There is a complimentary presence on a leap of faith to hold
      a desire strongly in your heart–mind,
trusting that for which you desire, comes into the seen from the
      unseen realm through expected
      and unexpected sources.
In this way, your belief factor muscle becomes stronger
and stronger
      to share and declare.
Each in a sense has their own intimate ministry to family,
friends,
      those mentored, and as well as businesspeople,
      the familiar,
      a chance meeting and beyond
      Pebbles in the Pond of Life —

Each causing a ripple in the larger body of living water,
      from there, one never knows to what shore
      it will arrive
once again, a universal pictorial of circles within circles.
      Outward bound circles and where they spread is
      the divine momentum, not yours to know
      or take any credit for, but to be faithful
      to toss forth the bread of life each day.

First within oneself, following guidance to care and share.
So it is, take satisfaction in this arena of activity.
Be a presence today and each day after first arising
and drinking
from the true well of inner waters.
Share the light of each day's blessings.
The ripples dance upon the pond to where
the unseen hand guides,
a lovely mystery
of which we are but a pebble in
the Great Pond of Life.

EMPTY

Talking about knowledge —
books stuffed into every corner
filled with facts, figures, inspiration and less.
Head filling for a crowded cranium
                                    yet feeling empty

Degrees framed neatly,
hung proudly on walls
titles and awards array
validation of knowledge earned
                                    yet feeling empty

Seminars, workshops, numerous retreats
prayer work, beads, toning, tapping
systems, mantras, crystals galore
yoga, walking, hiking, service and more
                                    yet feeling empty

Words of every kind float by —
computer, internet, television, CDs
phrases beautiful, poetic, demanding too,
NLP, NVC, on and on the learning spin
                                    yet, feeling empty

What is missing in the mental milieu?
Stuffed with knowledge of many forms
ancients, biblical, mystic, contemporary
bombarded on every side with more facts
                                    yet, feeling empty

Where is the stillness and rich silence?
Only hours of deep aloneness, contemplation
connecting to source of deeper understanding
distilling of knowledge into true Wisdom
                    a subtle filling

Touching the place that feels lost
healing parts that seem broken
poetry arises forming new inner life
balm touching the untouched, infusing
distilled knowledge becomes wisdom
                    no longer empty ... at last.

HALF-USED BED

What belonging is more intimate
    mythic, deeply personal
        than a bed?

Giving the gifts of comfort, sleep
    love making, dreaming
        than a bed?

Soft or firm, pliable the surface
    always awaiting, welcoming
        silently the bed.

Early in life it is one's first place
    staked out, this side or that
        familiar cozy bed.

When shared there are now two.
Severance now, only one alone
        changed awaits the bed.

Where to lay down the head
    to the left or the right
        strange now the bed.

Why must a choice be made
    spread wide, claim the available
        spacious bed.

Who knows or cares, none to witness
    sleep as you may choose
        in ever-present bed.

Yet often choosing the familiar side
    only half occupying the space
        holder of memories
            impartial bed.

FRAME AND RE-FRAME

Life art is the act of structuring being
often our gains disguised as loss.
Frame, then re-frame loss to potential gain
music improves as we fiddle.

Every end is a beginning.
Stalled for a while, new opening beckons,
getting unstuck from grief or loss
our balance improves.

Focusing on the loss, we look behind.
Almost missing our footing through pain,
timidly we look toward the future asking,
"How can this loss serve me?"

Learning to metabolize pain as energy
trusting again the life work we do,
walking through a different strange door,
a new day, new way, new dawn.

NEW PATH

Driving Route 1 to poetry workshop
    finding a place, I have never been.
        First solo drive, new experience, not going
        to stop.

An unexpected life, unattached and sad.
    Doing different things to broaden my life,
        A poetry retreat at beautiful spot can't be bad.

Hearing they have hot water pools which delight,
    never dreaming they still went nude …
        Horror! My first visit to baths hit like a spike.

Perspiration running down forehead.
    Nude with strangers in a public place?
        Or wear bathing suit, looking like fool instead?

Then through the door, my teacher, new,
    horrified, shy, perplexed a reaction.
        "Go away!" spontaneous spew.

Nothing to do but get over myself.
    Who really cares or is watching?
        No one of course, so towel on self.

Tightly clutched into shower warm,
    backside to world, front to majestic sea
        forgetting for a moment, just being norm.

Then the long walk, feeling a mature fool.
    Quiet time of day, visitors few
        edging to furthest hot water pool.

Easing into nature's medicinal gift.
    Clinging to rock walls, viewing sea,
        otters playing in sun-dappled joy ... a shift.

Becoming one with earth, sky and me.
    Tensions float away in bubbling swirls,
        at last, a barrier broken you see.

Patty Prude drowned in hot water pools.
    A more mature, self-activated woman
        arose from the waters of Esalen School.

LIFE IS A RIVER RAFT

Life is a river raft
over rapids
holding on
with all that is
                within me.

Waters not clean
from rivers of life
being splashed from waves
into face, eyes, mouth
spitting it out not swallowing
what could poison
                within me.

Contaminating my own well
drying my eyes to clear my vision
to see properly wiping
watery deposits
                off my face.

And having it come
again, and again, yet
not fall out of the raft, not
                swallow or drown.

There is an elation at the end
having survived intact,
grateful for courage
to take trip, ride, adventure
and not fall
out of raft.

Most joyous never
to do again this particular
soul journey on the
river of life.

All roads meet
all rivers flow into same sea
achieving perfection
through the imperfect gestures of
everyday life.

THE RIVER OF LIFE

The river of life, eternal stream
       sometimes the rapids
are fierce and wild,
       some season becalmed
       yet soft flowing.

There are times when
the river of life
is oh, so narrow,
       other moments so wide
       then vigorously flowing.

There are seasons of plenty,
       seasons of drought.
The river reflects an ever-changing
       unpredictable shifting scene
       that steadily keeps flowing.

There are times in our lives
       when the good times roll,
days when it is hard to live,
       ever-changing and shifting
       and breath keeps flowing.

So when we are becalmed
       in seemingly a forlorn place
when the torrents are too rapid
       or the flow not at all,
       remember, life is flowing.

Recalling the times
    when the river was wide
currents carrying us high
    the times being nowhere so low,
    deeply, the river kept flowing.

Tide comes in
    tide goes out.
The secret is to stay afloat.
    Hold firm for another day;
    the river she is a flowing...

Flowing, flowing
    with each breath
a new current begins.
    Hold on, dear one,
    the river of life carries you home.

DEEPEST SELF SINGING THE SONG
OF ONE'S BEING

A lull, a quiet receding of much activity, more a time of pause
        summer evokes lazy daze, yet lazy is a misnomer.
More a time of daydreaming, accessing deeper dreams,
hopes long
        ignored, nudges perhaps.
A time of cloud watching, discovering images and visions
produced by the
        constant etheric dance of molecules, vapors
        called wispy clouds.
Allowing the inner child out to play, stimulating
the imagination.
        From such fantasies have come great inventions,
        ideas that enriched humankind.

This is a time to lift the foot off the accelerator and coast,
swim if possible,
        muse, sketch, color, paint, write or just sit and stare,
formerly called the earliest meditation much like
the surfers do —
        gazing at the horizon awaiting the next set, lulled
        by the lapping
movement of the mighty ocean.
        Thoughts can often free float, and the inner voice
may speak to the heart-mind
        in the beauty and rhythmic waltz of the water.

Sometimes, a spiritual connection occurs, an awakening
        of the grandeur of something, someone larger
        than all of life,
certainty within the true self, a recognition that,
"I too am this,
        a part of the whole of creation."'
These are the golden moments of living where the egoic
arrogance humbly bows
        before a force of loving presence in the unification
        of oneness.
Yes, summer's hot, slow days can be a beautiful gift
of soft relaxation
        allowing the deepest self to sing the song of ones being.

ONE UNOBSERVED STEP AT A TIME

Thinking about things that cause me disquiet or anxiety.
These are feeding my pain body —
   sales already made without me
   all allegiances I cannot compel
   love that cannot be forced
The pain body is insidious in its dropping thoughts or
awakening situations
   in my memory causing painful revisiting.

What force within me wants to feed so rabidly?
What purpose in the divine makeup of being created in the
image and likeness
   of eternal divinity?
   The creator had a plan and a reason.
   I understand pain body desire for self-preservation
   and perpetuating
on the occurrences of life that evoke emotions and feelings
upon which it can feast.

Is it again the free choice that must be exercised, developed
to say "no we are not feasting
today on the unhappy, unfortunate things that could
happen in every life."
We shall feast on nourishing thoughts of all the goodness
that has come to us, me —
   all the blessed fortunate things
   all the love, travel, joy and laughter
   all the friends and lovely people populating
   my world.
Joy is the portion that feeds the soul.

Did Jesus leave his fellows when he too needed to wrestle
with the inner hardships of fear,
disappointment in the rejection of his beautiful life-
affirming message?
Forty days and nights of wrestling with so-called devil —
the liar, the deceiver
		who throws all your inadequacies
		your less than stellar behavior
		your outright mistakes
Into your face for a feeding frenzy.

How did he answer? Not with any rebuttal or condescending
to the accusations, but higher truth reframing the mistaken
impressions.
"I have bread you know not of."
Is the pain body a force, a work pulling humanity
into its lower self?
"The battle is not flesh and blood but principalities and
powers of darkness, to be overcome,
even within ourselves."

NEW MOON

New moon,
> I dream into you
> A new dream
> of a life more wonderful than it has ever been,
A love more vibrant,
> alive,
> exciting
> than yet experienced.
A time of creativity and expression
> far reaching
> in its excellence
> than yet produced.
A dance
> of miraculous savory
> depth, experiences
> and joy beyond great expectations.
A fruitful business
> flowing with new prosperity
> easily and effortlessly.
A time of new friendships
> communities
> involvement more enjoyable
> and productive
> then yet known.

A joyous,

      loving, travel-filled life

      that exceeds

      any adventures of the past,

      expanding perceptions,

      broadening awareness,

      deepening gratitude

      for this wonderful,

      fulfilling meaningful life.

Excitement builds as life gets better and better,

      more enjoyable with greater contribution

      then ever asked or hoped for.

Thank You, Loving Presence,

      Highest Wisdom,

      Greatest Good

      for touching this life today

      in a miraculous and marvelous way.

CHAPTER 7

THE JOURNEY WANES

A Road Never To Be Trod Again

THE HOURGLASS

The hourglass filled with sand
looks so full and forever
yet slowly, one grain at a time
sifting into passing days, nights, weeks, months, years.

Now more sand is in the spent portion
than reserved grains awaiting descent.
Almost immeasurable, the event of life's journey
comprised in more memories of days, weeks, months, years.

When the last particles of sand remain
and one is aware the pilgrimage is almost complete,
what footprints, monuments, remembrances
will testify to having inhabited this space

     of days, weeks, months, years ...
     decades?

BREATH

The breath is the precious gift
      not ours to keep,
only lent to manifest
      what life shall reap.

Then at the end of days
      that slow last breath retreats
going back to the source of all
      to give again, the cycle repeats.

There is only one breath.
      All breaths are the same cosmic breath,
ours to use as we choose during Earth walk
      until the moment departing, the breath slips away.

GRATEFUL HEART

Souls enter to grace life's play,
      live their lives by choice
or default,
      then exit the stage
leaving a hollow space
      in our hearts.

No one can quite fill that void
      seemingly belongs to no other.
Do our hearts finally look
      like Swiss cheese
punctured with losses unseen
      except by our hearts?

Grace, grace, sweet grace, the balm
      that heals the hurts
filling these punctures with
      love's memories,
gratitude that we once loved and laughed,
      treasures in our heart.

Thank you for touching our lives.
      Only gratitude for hours spent
can ease the sense of loss.
      Revisiting the joy shared
eases the emptiness echoing
      in vacant space.

Let's only remember the good
     tucked into our heart.
What would you say?
     I listen.

Thankfulness for all the
     sweetness of life is an acquired skill.
Taking time to celebrate
     the quiet miracles that seek no attention
enables an experience of holding each day
     as a sacred gift of wonder
held within the heart.

THE HOUSE OF SILENCE

The Pandemic 2020 - 2021

I now live in the house of silence
where once there were boisterous children.
Now the walls reverberate with soundlessness
in this season of my life. Where is the life of then?

I live in the silence now
mostly by choice, mine and the unseen forces.
I calculated and did not choose television
a long twenty years ago; I cannot bear the losses —

the losses of dignity, human life, and integrity,
the lies verbalized with such slick abandonment.
I enjoyed the silence while so busy stillness was fleeting
Yet now the pace has decreased, and in silence I ferment.

Hopefully, the fermentation will bring forth rich wine.
A time of being out of sight and curing as fine brew
which mellows and becomes rich and savory.
May this be the plan, a hope alluring.

In the proper time, the silence will be splintered
into a thousand rays of light
where once the noiselessness, with little stirring
a robust new life.

A life again filled with love and charm,
stirring with chosen ones abounding,
my rooms filled with joyous laughter ...
but for now, only my footfalls sounding.

I live in the house of silence
where deep listening is my goal,
a time away from frantic activity
for the enriching of my soul.

I live in the house of silence.
I have grown to appreciate it so,
unnecessary commotion and noise
makes me retreat with a "no."

The house of silence is awakened each day
with the song of the birds in the canyon,
the sunlight, though silent, dancing within,
and the wind chimes punctuate the beyond.

I live in the house of silence with my garden a riot.
If flowers could sing, a concerto would be heard
on a level far deeper than audio sound.
I give my ear to the song of wind, plants, and bird.

I live in the house of silence.
But my yard is alive with soft sounds.
If I listen carefully, the cricket, the deer
the caterpillar and frog, all make their rounds.

I live in the house of silence
by sweet choice.
Rejoice.

YIN ARISING WOMEN

You don't have to be a
    nipped, tucked, sucked
        bronzed, capped,
           dyed, coiffed
               California ideal woman.

You can be a lovely
    aging, yet beautiful
        maturing, authentic
           human being
               with softened breasts.

A natural face with character
    etched by the fingers
        of tears and laughter
           loving, losing, learning
               gained through courage.

To be real is to become
    transparent, a true beauty
        that rises from one's
           ground of being,
               graceful, elegant.

The inner terrain tended,
    cherished with gentle
        silence, solitude
           calm contemplation
               learning always.

Living out a richer
source of wealth
beyond glitz, golden bobbles
high-powered cars
designer frocks.

Being adorned with dignity
peace, poise, power
beyond the grasping
of the world's constant
hype and coercion.

Not being anything but your
true, intricate, multi-layered
unique self-kindness
the calling, healing the gift.

Wisdom distilled
from accumulated knowledge
is the stock in trade
under mentorship
of spiritual intelligence.

MY ONLY SON

Sixty some years ago, a boy child was born.
Behold a new life
as one who has been wide-eyed, inquiring,
challenging everything, all that is, was and is to come.

Sixty odd years ago, my life altered forever,
never the same
motherhood unprepared for such a soul
as this.

What karmic dance are we completing,
resolving or continuing?
These two colliding, loving, misunderstanding,
finding our own way.

Our cosmic star-crossed pairing —
mother, son, sister, brother
has forged a deepening, searching,
painful lessons, a spiritual odyssey.

Our greatest obstacles are often our greatest teachers.
Saints in beggar clothing
not being what they seemed,
the purifying fires bring forth gold.

Two ingots of refined metal
honed and shaped through union.
Relationships forge our inners
where that continuing unfolding
        reveals itself.

FRIENDS' FAREWELL

How precious are the hours,
days, months, years
yes, the moments
spent with a friend.

Human, of any age or size,
fur, feathers, or scales
the tender blessings
kind touch of a friend.

The connection deep and true
mutual enrichment
meaningful moments
in the presence of a friend.

Life is impermanent
on the physical level.
Love is eternal communion
for a dear friend.

Angels in skin, fur, feathers, or scales
a caring, a sharing
through time deepens
love for a friend.

Then comes the day
when we say farewell,
the physical gone
of that dear friend.

But the love is real
and lasts forever.
Energy never dies
remaining ever a friend.

Farewell, dear friend,
so precious to my heart
now in life we are apart
but always my friend.

Thank you for your life.

ONE SO SMALL WORD

One so small word
So large a concept,
Oneness of all life
Interconnected, a pure concept.

All small things that exist
Have come from the one source.
One breath of life animates all
Until the journey has run its course.

When returned to source,
energy runs to primary home,
not dead, just rearranged
to be distributed, newly honed.

Such is life, always creating
from itself, out of itself, into itself
The holy hoop of unending flow
changing expression yet remaining as self.

The long, dusty uncharted road
that climbs over oceans,
icebergs, rivers flow
day by day, prairie or plains singularly we go.

Seemingly separate yet united
individualized unique expression.
Yet at core, all the same
created to be individuals from one dimension.

This, a slow healing day, few steps to take
another run, jump, climb joyously
Others crowded about with clients, friends, family
But today, great quiet, listening, contemplation.

All these days make the tapestry,
some a little black, gray, brown hue,
another abundance of vivid colors, beautiful shades
swirled linear, horizontal, abstract,
making you, you!

VEIL PARTS

How does one share and not intrude?
How does one stand as a loving presence and not feel
the necessity to share their own truth
      or current truth as one knows it today?

So lightly does the veil part
and accepts the one with loving hands
who casting off the garment of the earth
      unto more celestial and peaceful lands.

That veil between realities, so thin
we live as if it does not in time,
and when the opening is for us,
      so quietly, that passage will be mine.

In saying farewell, never goodbye,
to cherished family and friends dear
in remembering the eternality of life,
      we will again see those once here.

The tears that may run down my face
this seemingly sad day will fade,
and joy again will be my way as I remember you
      and all the lovingly joy we made.

For we shall see all as they truly are
and they see us no longer through diffused glass.
For in the clarity of celestial light,
    we with helping, loving hands shall pass.

So, for today, dear one, I bid you farewell,
and some tomorrow unknown to me,
that long passage of light will call.
    And from Earth's journey, I shall be free.

Free at last, into the place from where I was lovingly created
by that one sweet divine energy of compassion.
Returning to family and friend,
    all sorrow now abated.

I AM ONE WITH ALL THAT IS

truth, stated in the simplest manner, affirms that
god is all there is.
    god never changes.
        god is in me.
            god is that which i am.

god is in the universe.
    god is the universe.
        no mediator exists between myself and god but my
        own thought.
            i am the writer, the inspirer, and the thing
            written about.
                i am the creator of history and the one
                who experiences it.
                    i am its record and
                    its interpretation.

"i am" is the thread of unity running through all, binding
us back to god.
    understanding god is perfect oneness; the fullness
    of god exists everywhere.
        "behold i stand at the door and knock."
            this divine visitor, which is my true self,
            is both the one
                who stands at the door and knocks,
                and the one who opens the door.
                    it is the glory of this recognition
                    that gives mastership.

there is but oneself who needs no mediator.
    this self is immediate, present, and available.
        every cell of my body, every thought of my mind,
        every glory
            of my spirit dwells in the very center
            of the One.
                in the stillness of a new day,
                    i know that I am one with all
                    there is,
                        now and always.

DEATH – DISAPPEARANCE

It has been said by a wise poet philosopher that fear of finality or death of the body is the dread of disappearance. Upon pondering this, I feel differently. The deep sense of an ongoing existence is so real to me that death, though I am not welcoming it at this time, is not so fearful. And the thought of disappearance is not even in the equation. My thoughts rather ran like this:

Fear of disappearing? Perhaps not.
    More the riveting disappointment
    of not accomplishing
        those visual stirrings deep within
          wanting exposure.
Oh, the greatest gift in this graying season
    is the ever-elusive gift,
        that is said to be illusionary construct —
        time.

Time is the gift of wanting,
    not a stillborn, but vital expression.
A stillborn of all that might have, could have been,
    so late the fetus stirs within
        pleading for life experience.

A visible voice
    shall capricious time allow
        this long incubating birth?

DEATH AND AWAKENING

Our beloveds are not dead.
Those we have embraced to our breast
have found sweet peace and quiet rest.
They live and move among the blessed.

They are not dead.
Beyond Earth's slowly setting sun,
another life has just begun,
another course of action to run.

They are not dead.
Beyond Earth's storms, mists and rain
beyond all sorrow, fear and pain
new life, new joy, shall spring again.

They are not dead.
They have but found new songs to sing
new life and laughter there to bring
to love more fully in the eternal spring.

Your dear one is not dead.
That energy has only changed form.
seeing and knowing you still,
ever watching over you, dear ones.

FOOTPRINTS

No one walks the sands of time unnoticed.
> "Oh," you say, "the tide comes in and washes away
> my imprint in the sand, and
> none will remember I walked this way."

The sand knows and felt your weight.
> The ocean waters remember as it washes
> over your individualized print
> momentarily sculpting the wet shoreline.

The air remembers your fragrance,
> the sky testifies to your light,
> captured and embedded
> in the stars of the night.

None walks alone
> down the dusty red road.
> "Oh," you say, "the winds blow
> and my print disappears."

The rains come
> and wash in tiny rivulets,
> every trace of my traveling life's road
> far from sight.

But the dust that dances
> upon the breeze
> carries your energy,
> the rain that washes

Over the Earth
> captures within each rainbow drop,
> a remembrance
> of you.

Your song is sung in the wind
        and your smile
        reflects in each glistening
        dew-kissed flower.

Your silence calms
        the agitated air,
        your sweetness
        scents the pungent
        aroma of the earth,

And your essence
        reverberates throughout
        the vast spheres
        forever
        and ever!

Though not seen as you were,
        you are remembered today
        and each day when the sun shines
        and the waves lap upon the shore

And the breeze stirs the red earth,
        and each dew drop,
every rain puddle glistening,
your love is alive.

Your imprint remains
        eternally
        in the energy that never,
        ever ceases.

Sweet journey, Dear One —
        Until your loved ones meet you again
        and again
        and again ...

DEAR ONES REJOICE — A FAREWELL POEM

Where has she gone?
    Her envelope of flesh
        still and cool

Her smile welcoming
    not now present
        a silence startling

Her laughter lingering
    in many memories dear
        no longer ours to hear

The helping hands still
    resting in repose
        no longer responsive to her will

The slim trim body
    in eternal sleep
        no new steps to seek

The road has ended
    she quietly writes a new page
        with angels long befriended

Companions all of her life
    whispering caring lovingly
        in travels, family, joys and strife

She has returned to the originality of it all
    her walk wrote her story
        gifting her with a farewell poem

Not now, but someday.

BIRTHING OF A BOOK

Wondering, pondering, embracing the unknown,
    carrying an unborn child for many long months is
        one of the deepest journeys into inquiry

Wondering, is it a boy or a girl
    Will it be healthy
        Am I up to task of motherhood

Wonderings, many various, just below the surface
    thoughts of excitement and anticipated joy
        names, clothes, gender, numerous unknowns

Towards the end the anxiousness of a swollen
    bulging being where once one was
        slim, trim, fit and supple

These same feelings beginning once more,
    the emotional pondering of a long pregnancy
        bringing forth a collection of poetry
        into the light of day

I am told a book takes on a life of its own,
    just like a child it becomes something in its own right.
        I am feeling stark naked before unknown eyes
Intended just for family and few friends it has developed
    into a missile of its own to be sent forth into
    the larger world
        now being unattached, severed like
        an umbilical cord

Wondering, unsure but unable to now abandon the process,
    may it find its way into the hearts and minds for
    whom it is meant
        to touch, inspire or aid in expansion of their
        own inner life

Has been my silent prayer
                     — *Mystic Cloud Walker*

ARTISTS' ACKNOWLEDGEMENTS

These are paintings I collected through the years that have significant meaning to me, which are reflected in some of my poetry. It is with gratitude for the artistic community in which I live and from my travels that these beautiful souls dedicate their lives to enhancing our experience through their ever-creative eyes.

Cover:
"Mystic Cloud Walker" ®
Digital creation by Jerry Wayne Downs

Chapter 1:
"Cloud on a String" by Jerry Wayne Downs

Chapter 2:
"A Laguna Day" by Jerry Wayne Downs

Chapter 3:
"Painting of the Author" by Marianne Van Der Veer

Chapter 4:
"Author's Feet" photo, Laguna Beach, California

Chapter 5:
(Portals) "Portals" by Jeff Peters
(Passage) "Illumination: Star of the Sea"
by David Begley

Chapter 6:
"Cambodia, Burma" by Jerry Wayne Downs

Chapter 7:
"The Novel" by Jerry Wayne Downs

JERRY WAYNE DOWNS is a prolific and imaginative artist who uses many differing expressions — futuristic worlds, portraits, commission pieces, land and seascapes, surrealism, and also romantic dream-like atmospheres, all ripping through the veil of conventionality, and prompting questions about the fragility of our present. A former animator for Disney, his experience and style bring enchantment to his works.

JerryDowns44@gmail.com

DAVID BEGLEY works in many mediums. His drawings, paintings and prints are shown in galleries and festivals in Australia, China, Germany, Greece, Italy, the United States, the United Kingdom and Ireland, where he resides. I saw his work in a lovely gallery in Dublin, and his detailed exquisite painting would not let me leave the country without purchasing it. It has influenced "Passages" with a lovely emotional visual for deep feelings and words that were to tumble onto the page.

davidbegleyartist@gmail.com

Instagram.com/davidbegleyartist

Facebook.com/davidbegleyartist

MARIANNE VAN DER VEER was born in the Netherlands. She began her art training at a young age at the Gerrit Rietveld Academy in Amsterdam. It encompassed fine art painting, graphics, and interior design. In America, she furthered her extensive training at Art Center College in Los Angeles. She is a portrait artist, muralist, and does commission pieces of individuals and their beloved pets. She also teaches. She has lived in numerous places in Europe, including France and Switzerland, and United Arab Emirates and other parts of the Middle East. She currently resides in Laguna Beach.

www.myanderveer.com

mvanderveer7@gmail.com

JEFF PETERS is a painter and illustrator known for his figurative paintings and his detailed intricate brushwork and themes of nature, which take a leap into the realm of ideal. He is diversified in his artistic expressions combining romanticism with collage art and paintings reconciling his immediate surrounds with perfect, supple, and unique coloration. He is collected nationally, with exhibits in Los Angeles and Laguna Beach, and in museums such as Irvine Fine Arts Center, California State University, and Center Club in Newport Beach. He attended Laguna College of Art & Design.
IAmJeffPeters@gmail.com

GAIL RIENA MICHAEL is an editor who has worked with and encouraged writers with their papers, screenplays, novels, autobiographies, and books of poetry. Her goal is to assist them with putting into words what they want to share with the world and help them achieve their dream of becoming a published author. She is also a ghost writer and writer who has published three novels and e-books, articles, poetry, and was a co-author in the *Giving Gratitude–Wake Up Live the Life You Love* series.
Capri383@gmail.com

ABOUT THE AUTHOR

Patricia P. Truman has been an active businesswoman for 41-plus years. She was in banking then became a certified Escrow Officer, eventually originating and running the escrow company for Laguna Niguel Corporation.

After a childbearing retirement, she became active in philanthropic endeavors and was also a professional model for many years. Returning to the business world, she obtained her real estate license, becoming a top producer and Realtor of the Year in 2008; she is still active in the business world.

Later, she obtained her ministerial license and became a staff minister, where she performed spiritual counseling, participated as a prayer practitioner, and was a well-received teacher of numerous classes through Centers for Spiritual Living. She was ordained in 2012 and is still active, facilitating small groups, speaking, writing, and performing rituals including weddings, christenings, and memorial services.

Patricia is deeply committed to her large, ever-expanding family. As a world traveler who has visited numerous sacred sites, which are her passion, she has explored many countries around our diverse and beautiful planet. Their reflections are often caught in her poetry, essays and prose pieces.

She has been published in *Creative Thought* magazine and other print publications. This book is her first public appearance in the literary arts.

Facebook: www.facebook.com/patriciapepertruman
Website: patriciatruman.com

Made in the USA
Middletown, DE
25 February 2022